The Liberal Arts in Higher Education

Challenging Assumptions, Exploring Possibilities

Edited by

Diana Glyer

David L. Weeks

University Press of America, Inc.
Lanham • New York • Oxford

University Press of America,® Inc.
4720 Boston Way
Lanham, Maryland 20706

12 Hid's Copse Rd.
Cummor Hill, Oxford OX2 9JJ

Printed in the United States of America
British Library Cataloging in Publication Information Available

Library of Congress Cataloging-in-Publication Data

The liberal arts in higher education : challenging assumptions, exploring possibilities / edited by Diana Glyer, David L. Weeks.
p. cm.
Includes bibliographical references and index.
1. Education, Humanistic. 2. Education, Humanistic—United States. 3. Education, Higher—Aims and objectives. 4. Education, Higher—Aims and objectives—United States. I. Glyer, Diana. II. Weeks, David L.
LC1011.L455 1998 370.11'2—dc21 98-22991 CIP

ISBN 0-7618-1164-8 (pbk: alk. ppr.)

™ The paper used in this publication meets the minimum requirements of American National Standard for Information Sciences—Permanence of Paper for Printed Library Materials, ANSI Z39.48—1984

Contents

Part One: The Articles

Part Two: The Reviews

Foreword

The challenge of providing a quality education has never been greater. We live in a time of unparalleled growth in a world of unparalleled need—and conscientious educators are wise to devote serious thought to the kind of university that will best prepare this generation for such a time and place.

At the heart of such discussion must be a clear understanding of the liberal arts, those subjects which strive to educate the whole person. As we are often reminded, a successful liberal education prepares students not for a specific profession but for life itself, for the moral, intellectual, social, civic, and spiritual growth that accompany a life well-lived. The liberal arts have a central place in the curriculum at Azusa Pacific University, as they have always had at leading universities.

Given such a prominent position and lofty purpose, one might expect that the nature of the liberal arts in higher education would be easy to describe and straightforward to implement. However, as David Weeks and Diana Glyer remind us in their thoughtful introduction, these questions have become increasingly muddied by the passage of time and the emergence of competing priorities. That is why a volume such as this one is timely and important. The essays and reviews here do more than showcase the considerable talent of the faculty at APU: they provide a clear, uncompromising treatment of one of the most important issues of our day.

Are the liberal arts necessary? Is liberal education really important? Looking back as well as forward, H. G. Wells reminds us that "Human history becomes more and more a race between education and catastrophe." This book provides a substantial starting point for dialogue about what is the proper foundation of higher education. I commend it to you with enthusiasm and high hope.

Richard E. Felix, Ph.D.
President
Azusa Pacific University

Acknowledgments

Producing a book incurs many debts. We are grateful for the many teachers and colleagues who have inspired our interest in liberal education and who have shaped our thinking on the topic. We specifically want to acknowledge the faculty authors of the articles and reviews. We appreciate their toleration of our persistence and niggling. They are colleagues in the very best sense of the word. The introduction was vastly improved by the careful, detailed reading of reviewers James Hedges, Alan Padgett, and Christopher Flannery. We appreciate their time, energy, and insight and absolve them of any responsibility for remaining error, obfuscation, or confusion. Yuka Sudo and David McGill served as creative consultants on the cover design. Our able assistant, Adrienne Miller, has tracked down innumerable sources, followed-up on infinite detail, mastered the intricacies of *The Chicago Manual of Style*, and kept us on track throughout the project. Elva Rimington displayed her usual virtuosity, resourcefulness, and undying support on this project. Jane Thorndike tracked down numerous sources.

We are truly grateful for the editorial assistance and professionalism of Nancy Ulrich and Helen Hudson, the expertise and typesetting of Dorothy Albritton, and the outstanding copyediting of Georgeann Halburian Ikuma. The book was enriched by the special effort of APU's Office of University Marketing and Creative Media, especially David Peck, Virginia Carter, Carmen Gustin, and Maureen Riegert Foley. We are indebted to Azusa Pacific University's administration for their support and financial assistance: Richard E. Felix, Jon Wallace, Patricia S. Anderson, Clifford Hamlow, Hank C. Bode, and David Bixby.

Most importantly, we thank our families for putting up with long hours and periods of neglect and distraction. Mike, Debbie, Christopher, and Mitchell are our greatest sources of support, inspiration, and happiness. God has truly blessed us by bringing them into our lives.

Liberal Education: Initiating the Conversation

by Diana Glyer and David L. Weeks

What are the liberal arts? What is liberal education? Basic questions—yet they have perplexed, challenged, and confounded educators for nearly twenty-five hundred years. Efforts to clarify the contours of the liberal arts and liberal education have long been animated by disagreements between philosophers and rhetoricians, pagans and Christians, ancients and moderns. These creative tensions still exist and are compounded by new developments: the advent of modern science, the effects of classical and contemporary liberalism, the influence of pragmatism, the predominance of the German research university model, the explosion of professional education, the emergence of postmodernism, the challenge of multiculturalism, and the rising tide of political conservatism.

Nonetheless, liberal education, the chief educational aim since the time of Socrates, has survived, even thrived, and has retained respect and admiration. Educators invoke the phrase for virtually every heartfelt

---

DIANA GLYER is an associate professor of English in the College of Liberal Arts and Sciences at Azusa Pacific University. She is a graduate of Bowling Green State University (B.A., B.S.), Northern Illinois University (M.S.), and University of Illinois at Chicago (Ph.D.). **DAVID L. WEEKS** is professor of political science and dean of the College of Liberal Arts and Sciences at Azusa Pacific University. He is a graduate of Indiana Wesleyan University (B.S.), Indiana State University (M.A.), and Loyola University of Chicago (Ph.D.).

educational objective. Such widespread usage of the term liberal education becomes problematic when incompatible aims are identified with it. Does liberal education foster independence or interdependence, look to the past or the future, develop national identity or global citizenship, promote unity or diversity, cultivate moral or intellectual virtue, address urgent social problems or timeless human dilemmas, help students understand the world or motivate them to change it, inculcate respect for eternal verities or nurture a spirit of skepticism, lead to personal introspection or promote social action? Is liberal education concerned with the transmission of knowledge or with the advancement of knowledge? Is it elitist and aristocratic or egalitarian and democratic? Is it preparatory or an end in itself, an introduction to different disciplines or interdisciplinary, preparation for specialization or a counterbalance to specialization?

The literature suggests liberal education does all of these things and more. On closer examination, however, these educational aims, each one valid in its own right, are not easily reconciled. Perhaps such tensions are part and parcel of liberal education, paradoxes that keep the debate from degenerating into meaningless oversimplification. But it is also possible that these broad goals are antithetical, competitive, and irreconcilable. For example, is liberal education's penchant for liberty compatible with respect and toleration of frankly non-democratic views? If liberal education is primarily the cultivation of intellectual capacity, is it not inherently elitist, since only a few possess superior genius? Does encouraging students to "think for themselves" lead to a conscious, self-assertive resistance to authority that undermines cooperation and community? Do calls to redress urgent social ills reorient the focus of liberal education from ends to means, thus inviting the idolatry of ideology?[1] Why study the humanities if the goal is sharpening the critical intellect, which one might argue is best done by mathematical and natural sciences? Does fostering a radical spirit of questioning undermine the establishment of moral principle?

---

[1]According to Eva Brann, "An ideology is a rational theory that is no longer in the state of inquiry; it is rather an accepted teaching to which the totality of actions and opinions is expected to conform, a theory 'intended to change the world, not interpret it.'" *Paradoxes of Education in a Republic* (Chicago, IL: University of Chicago Press, 1979), 39.

These questions are particularly germane at our institution, Azusa Pacific University, a coeducational, Christian, comprehensive university located in Southern California. Founded in 1899 as the Training School for Christian Workers, the school has gone through several metamorphoses and now serves more than 5,000 undergraduate and graduate students. Entrepreneurial and innovative, APU has enjoyed substantial growth, financial stability, and widening recognition. These developments were applauded by Ernest L. Boyer who served on a Carnegie Foundation visitation team and later wrote: "Azusa Pacific University is becoming a leader among colleges and universities willing to combine an unapologetic commitment to Christianity with an uncompromising commitment to educational excellence."[2]

This does not mean that difficulties do not remain. Explosive growth prompts introspection. Who are we? What are we doing? Why? What educational purpose(s) do we serve? One of APU's most interesting challenges is shared with hundreds of other colleges and universities: the challenge of carving out an identity as a comprehensive university that offers both professional preparation and a liberal education.[3] This dual mission requires a clear understanding of both enterprises, and a manner of pursuing each that is not indifferent or antithetical to the other. Our constituencies, as well as our mission statement, require no less.

This book is intended to spark a conversation about liberal education on our campus. In this respect, the book has a specific addressee, the Azusa Pacific University community. Nonetheless, we share its contents with the hope that it might serve a similar purpose elsewhere.

In order for such a conversation to be both substantive and constructive, we believe that it must be preceded by three things: (1) clarity about key terminology; (2) reflection upon the often unarticulated presuppositions behind various paradigms of liberal education; and (3) a clear statement of the perennial debates about the content of liberal education. Those are

---

[2]"A Community of Teaching and Learning: Striking the Balance," report to Azusa Pacific University (The Carnegie Foundation for the Advancement of Teaching, December 1988), 3.

[3]Comprehensive universities often lack the clear identity of liberal arts colleges, major research universities, and local community colleges.

the goals of this introduction. This volume continues the conversation by offering four essays that explore various aspects of this issue, and a series of critical reviews of some of the most quoted literature on the topic.

The Challenge of Defining Liberal Education

Why is it so difficult to clearly define the idea of a liberal education? The short answer, we believe, is because of decades of fuzzy thinking on the topic. Confusion has resulted from competing paradigms, ambiguous language, and a desire to co-opt the concept of liberal education in support of various educational visions. As a result, nearly every institution of higher education invokes the idea of liberal education but few institutions define it with precision. Those who have received acclaim for defining it do so differently—contrast, for example, St. John's effort to sharpen the mind through study of great books to Alverno's intent to strengthen measurable competencies.

This state of affairs is not new. The ambiguity has persisted for so long in so many quarters that we are reluctant to confront the issue. But the need for clear definition gains new urgency during a time when higher education is increasingly called upon to give an account of itself. The implicit challenge is that only those components of higher education which readily demonstrate their intrinsic worth or utility will survive. It is difficult to demonstrate the worth and, perhaps, utility of liberal education if one cannot clearly delineate what it is. A muddled mission makes it more difficult to justify the expenditure of scarce resources, more difficult to summon commitment on the part of faculty and students, and more difficult to assess the success or failure of the endeavor.

This lack of clarity has been noted in virtually every decade of the 1900s. Near the turn of the century, a college president lamented, "The college is without clear-cut notions of what a liberal education is and how it is to be secured, . . . and the pity of it is that this is not a local or special disability, but a paralysis affecting every college of arts in America." Approaching mid-century, scholars were saying, "there is little agreement about what liberal education should be," the "theory and practice [of liberal education] are confused and contradictory," and "the most striking thing about the higher learning in America is the confusion that besets it." One observer noted that "liberal arts faculties seldom state clearly what they mean by liberal or general education" and surmised "perhaps they do not know." Twenty years ago, a commentator noted that "liberal education has become splintered, specialized, and, to some extent, eroded," that it lacked coherence, and defied clear definition. More recently, a prominent student of higher education concluded that "we do not really understand what we mean when we invoke (as we often do) the phrase 'liberal education.'"[4] It simply means whatever we want it to mean at the moment we utter the phrase or, worse yet, it means everything and nothing.

For purposes of this discussion, we offer the following working definitions of key terms:

- ***Liberal Arts***: although the notion of academic disciplines is a recent development, seven fields of study have historically been identified as liberal arts: logic, grammar, rhetoric, mathematics, geometry, music, and astronomy. Any number of other subjects have been dubbed modern spin-offs of those seven fields, but there is no consensus about other fields claiming such status.
- ***Liberal Education***: an education grounded in the liberal arts which extends to an investigation into the central human questions: Who am I? Why am I here? What is my responsibility to God, to other individuals, to the community?

---

[4]Quotations can be found in Abraham Flexner, *The American College: A Criticism* (New York, NY: Century, 1908), 7; Thomas Woody, *Liberal Education for Free Men* (Philadelphia, PA: University of Pennsylvania Press, 1951), 222; Robert Maynard Hutchins, *The Higher Learning in America* (New Haven, CT: Yale University Press, 1936; reprint, with an introduction by Harry S. Ashmore, New Brunswick, NJ: Transaction Publishers, 1995), 1; Bruce A. Kimball, *Orators and Philosophers: A History of the Idea of Liberal Education,* expanded edition (New York, NY: College Entrance Examination Board, 1995), 196; Earl F. Cheit, *The Useful Arts and the Liberal Tradition* (New York, NY: McGraw-Hill, 1975), 136; and Joseph L. Featherstone, "Foreword," to Bruce A. Kimball, *Orators and Philosophers,* xvii.

What is true? What is good? What is beautiful? It is also helpful to explain what liberal education is not. The following three views may be part of liberal education but should not be mistaken for liberal education itself: (1) the development of transferable intellectual capacities (critical thinking, higher-order reasoning, intellectual virtue) and the sharpening of basic skills (reading, writing, speaking, listening);[5] (2) a survey of the "cultural heritage of Western civilization" to establish cultural literacy, inculcate Western values, and cultivate aesthetic taste;[6] and (3) general education (see below).[7]

- ***Trivium***: those disciplines generally referred to as the literary arts, the verbal arts, the humane letters, the arts of eloquence—grammar, logic, and rhetoric. These protean arts were always understood more broadly than contemporary formulations; the trivium generally included but was never restricted to linguistics, critical thinking, and persuasive communication, the arts of composing, delivering, and analyzing written and oral communication, or even reading, writing, and thinking.

---

[5]A wonderful early expression of this view is found in the Yale Report of 1828. "The two great points to be gained in intellectual culture are the *discipline* and *furniture* of the mind; expanding its powers, and storing it with knowledge. The former of these is, perhaps, the more important of the two. A commanding object, therefore, in a collegiate course, should be, to call into daily and vigorous exercise the faculties of the student. Those branches of study should be prescribed, and those modes of instruction adopted, which are best calculated to teach the art of fixing the attention, directing the train of thought, analyzing a subject proposed for investigation; following, with accurate discrimination, the course of the argument; balancing nicely the evidence presented to the judgment; awakening, elevating, and controlling the imagination; arranging, with skill, the treasures which memory gathers; rousing and guiding the powers of genius." Richard Hofstadter and Wilson Smith, eds., *American Higher Education: A Documentary History* (Chicago, IL: University of Chicago Press, 1961), 1:278.

[6]Carnegie Foundation for the Advancement of Teaching, *Missions of the College Curriculum* (San Francisco, CA: Jossey-Bass, 1978), 3, 9.

[7]Synonymous use of liberal education and general education has probably contributed more confusion to recent discussion than any other development. Bell, Hutchins, Meiklejohn, Thomas, and the Harvard Report equate the terms. Van Doren, Miller, and Boyer maintain a distinction.

It was not accidental that one studied the arts of eloquence by reading classical literature, often histories, not only in one's native language, but in a foreign language (usually Latin and Greek) because the classics were the consummate guide to moral philosophy (ethics and politics). Therefore, a contemporary formulation of the trivium probably includes the study of language, literature, foreign language, communication, logic, history, ethics, and politics.

- ***Quadrivium***: those disciplines often referred to as the mathematical arts, the arts of wisdom and understanding—arithmetic, geometry, music, and astronomy. These arts revolve around the study of things, of quantities, and of abstractions, symbolic representations of things such as numbers. One scholar describes the quadrivium as consisting "of the mathematical or 'learnable' arts, so called because they concern intelligible objects, which are traditionally ordered according to increasing corporeality, from dimensionless arithmetic through plane and solid geometry, to astronomy (the application of mathematics to moving bodies) and music (the study of bodies executing harmonious motions, that is, physics)."[8] Geography was often a part of the study of geometry. A contemporary formulation of the quadrivium probably includes mathematics, the natural sciences (physics, astronomy, geology, biology, and chemistry) and, perhaps, geography.
- ***Liberalism***: those modern social and political movements ranging from democratic socialists to libertarians which are identified with the ideals of liberty, equality, progress, and individual rights. Although both classical and contemporary liberals advance particular and influential understandings of

---

[8]Brann, *Paradoxes of Education in a Republic*, 119.

liberal education, liberalism and liberal education are not essentially related. Political liberals are not the end product of liberal education.

- ***General Education***: an utterly amorphous notion that is used to describe either (a) an educational experience that prepares all students for life in general, a common denominator approach;[9] or (b) a basic level of study in most major fields of inquiry, that is to say, a required "taste" of many different fields; or (c) a comprehensive term used to describe the combination of academic and co-curricular experiences that constitute a student's complete college experience.

These working definitions, which reveal our viewpoint, serve as a basis for a campuswide conversation. The theoretical origins and practical implications of these definitions become clearer when discussed in conjunction with the broader and more fundamental topic of educational paradigms.

Liberal Education Paradigms

Clarifying definitions requires, in part, study of the etymological origins and historical development of terms. It also requires investigation into how the terms are used within various paradigms of liberal education and reflection upon their often unarticulated presuppositions. A fair explication of the ideas, assumptions, and arguments of major educational traditions is a tremendous aid to understanding liberal education. It helps

---

[9]This typically means life in contemporary society. "General education undertakes to redefine liberal education in terms of life's problems as men face them, to give it human orientation and social direction, to invest it with content that is directly relevant to the demands of contemporary society. General education is liberal education with its matter and method shifted from its original aristocratic intent to the service of democracy. General education seeks to extend to all men the benefits of an education that liberates." "The President's Commission on Higher Education for Democracy, 1947," in Hofstadter and Smith, eds., *American Higher Education: A Documentary History*, 2:990.

us appreciate the intellectual coherence of various paradigms and grapple with the inherent contradictions among them.

It seems to us that such a study would, at least, focus on the four major paradigms which are the sources of many claims and platitudes frequently reiterated in contemporary discussions of liberal education. Although no one person, institution, or document fully embodies any single paradigm, each represents the position of many people.

A. *The Classical Greek Philosophic Tradition.* The dominant paradigm in liberal education is the classical Greek model. Beginning with the assumption that truth is both universal and accessible, this model emphasizes the pursuit of truth for its own sake. A sense of awe or wonder about the nature of things inspires the quest for understanding wholly apart from utility. Speculative, contemplative, reflective, teleological, the Greek tradition emphasizes wisdom, understanding, first principles, ends rather than means. Because reason is the unique human capacity which enables one to know the truth and emancipates humanity from mere opinion, the cultivation of reason is the aim of education. The educational enterprise culminates in philosophy, the dialectic. Plato's powerful image of escape from the darkness of a cave to the splendor of light is an apt metaphor; the light of reason disperses darkness and enables the inquiring mind to see the good, the true, the beautiful.

B. *The Humanistic Tradition.* The humanistic tradition greatly admires the accomplishments of the classical Greek mind. Recognizing, however, the impracticality and contingency of an unsettling and endless quest for knowledge, humanists place less emphasis on freeing the mind and more emphasis on making people fit for freedom. Moral virtue and civic virtue become the aim of education. Education entails the transmission of knowledge and culminates, not in philosophy, but in literature. In literature, one finds the greatest expression of human understanding, human experience, and human achievement. From a careful reading of great works, one collects pearls of wisdom which enable one to be a good person—cultivated, civilized, and courteous—and, more importantly, a good citizen.[10]

C. *Modernity's Scientific Paradigm.* Sharing antiquity's faith in the capacity of human reason, modern thinkers turn their attention from the heavens to the earth, from the eternal to the temporal, from the soul to the body. The aim of modern inquiry was progress, defined as the "relief of man's estate."[11] The means to that end is the scientific method which promised to liberate humanity from enslaving impersonal forces by ferreting out those laws of nature which govern the material universe and turning them to our advantage. Education plays a key role in this revolution by training the specialist, the researcher, the scientist. Understanding "liberal" to mean "liberating from constraint," liberal educators turn attention away from the transmission of knowledge to the discovery of knowledge. The humanities are shunned as subjective expressions of personal opinion, and the experimental sciences become pre-eminent because of their allegedly neutral, objective methodology. Study of the sciences, it is claimed, hones the intellect and requires mastery of modes of inquiry, thus preparing students for the specialization that is required in the quest to master the forces of nature. Moreover, the sciences are founded upon an optimism that progress will result from human inquiry, and they foster a healthy spirit of tolerance and skepticism, for all discoveries are susceptible to revision.

D. *The Twentieth-Century Pragmatic Vision.* Inflating the inherited epistemological skepticism of modernity, twentieth-century thinkers

---

[10]In *Essay on Modern Education*, Jonathan Swift writes, "The books read at school and college are full of incitements to virtue, and discouragements from vice, drawn from the wisest reasons, the strongest motives, and the most influencing examples. Thus young minds are filled with an inclination to good and an abhorrence of evil, both of which increase in them, according to the advances they make in literature." Quoted in Martin L. Clarke, *Classical Education in Britain, 1500-1900* (Cambridge: Cambridge University Press, 1959), 169.

[11]Francis Bacon in *Advancement of Learning and Novum Organum* (New York, NY: Willey, 1900), bk. 1, c. 5, sect. 11.

become increasingly dubious about any truth claim, especially metaphysical claims.[12] Metaphysical agnosticism results: if truth is elusive, contingent, and subjective, then value judgments depend wholly on context and perspective. Because the human perspective is ultimately derived from social context, human affairs and the needs of the community become the abiding concern. Practical reason, problem solving, and social progress become the foci of liberal education, understood as a liberalizing force. Increasingly defined as general education, liberal education becomes preparation for the demands of contemporary society. The goal is not to understand the world but to change it, to actualize human potential, to free all peoples from oppressive, inherited traditions, ideas, and practices based on spurious truth claims. As such, liberal education no longer culminates in philosophical speculation, scientific inquiry, or humanistic reflection, but in social studies. The social sciences illuminate individual behavior, provide insight into social relations, and help devise a better world. The future shall be better than the past if we address the needs of existing community life, finding common values and a sense of community in an increasingly pluralistic, multicultural society.

The pragmatic vision offers, as do the other three paradigms, a comprehensive and intellectually coherent understanding of the educational

---

[12]We use the label "pragmatic" for lack of a better term. Bruce Kimball insists that the "resurgent intellectual tradition of pragmatism" is the dominant, if unnoticed, force in higher education today. Kimball summarizes his understanding of this movement, which some observers describe as postmodernism, with six themes. "These themes are (1) that belief and meaning, even truth itself, are fallible and revisable; (2) that an experimental method of inquiry obtains in all science and reflective thought; (3) that belief, meaning, and truth depend on the context and the intersubjective judgment of the community in which they are formed; (4) that experience is the dynamic interaction of organism and environment, resulting in a close interrelationship between thought and action; (5) that the purpose of resolving doubts or solving problems is intrinsic to all thought and inquiry; and (6) that all inquiry and thought are evaluative, and judgments about fact are not different from judgments about value." Bruce Kimball, "Toward Pragmatic Liberal Education," in *The Condition of American Liberal Education*, ed., Robert Orrill (New York, NY: College Board Publications, 1995), 83. He argues convincingly that virtually every major recent development in liberal education (multiculturalism, service learning, pluralism, interdisciplinary studies, learner-centered teaching, assessment) can be logically explained by this resurgent pragmatism.

enterprise. Learning more about all of these paradigms should enrich debate about liberal education.

Perennial Debates

The aforementioned paradigms provide background and insight into many contemporary debates about liberal education. At APU, we are concerned, among other things, with a Christian perspective on liberal education. There is no single Christian perspective because Christian thinkers have borrowed extensively from the other traditions, especially the classical Greek and humanistic traditions, although vestiges of the modern scientific and pragmatic can be found in current formulations. Historically, Christians sought to foster both moral and intellectual virtue—intellectual virtue to understand God's truth; moral virtue to abide by God's will—by reading texts from the Church Fathers. Wary of pagan teaching, Christians also gingerly selected those pagan texts which appeared to have escaped the taint of sin and offered insight into truth and virtue. The study of the liberal arts always culminated in the study of Scripture. For in Scripture, we find the truth that sets us free.

Concern for a Christian perspective may be unique to Christian colleges and universities, but we face other issues that exist on every college campus. Five of these issues seem particularly important. We briefly review those perennial debates, not to resolve the issues but to bring them to the forefront of conversation.

A. ***Moral v. Intellectual Virtue.*** Does a liberal education contribute to both intellectual and moral virtue? It is commonplace to assert that a liberal education sharpens the critical intellect. But will it strengthen moral virtue? The humanistic tradition thought so. The study of classical literature with its portrayal of heroic figures struggling with moral choices was seen as central to a moral education. If one understands the choices with all their personal and social ramifications, then one is more likely to choose well. However, some thinkers sharply distinguish the mind from the will, and therefore, assert that sharpening the mind, their idea of liberal education's aim, has little to do with making good moral choices.[13] Others argue that "any radical disjunction of moral education and intellectual education is perilous."[14]

Is liberal education a moral enterprise? Should it "develop the reasoning faculties of our youth" as well as "instill into them the precepts of virtue and order?"[15] If so, how do we shape the moral character of students? Whose morals do we choose to inculcate, and when moral imperatives conflict, what mechanism do we use to choose between them? Is intellectual virtue possible without moral virtue? Each institution which stakes a claim to liberal education should be prepared to provide answers.

B. *Science v. the Humanities.* What are the disciplinary emphases of a liberal arts education? Historically, the relative peace that has been achieved about the curriculum has been rife with differences. Some educators adopt an "oratorical vision of liberal education," emphasizing the arts of language and literature. Other thinkers dismiss this as imprecise and incapable of discerning truth. "These 'philosophers' search for a precise, rational method of pursing knowledge" and regard the arts of wisdom, the mathematical arts, as the key to a liberal arts education.[16]

Today, this often heated debate continues under the guise of "the battle of the books." Which grouping of disciplines, the humanities or the sciences, are most likely to foster liberal education? This debate was fought with great finesse in the late 1800s by two friends: Matthew

---

[13]For example, Mortimer Adler claims, "The contribution that can be made by higher education is mainly limited to the sphere of the intellectual virtues." "Education and the Pursuit of Happiness," in *Reforming Education: The Opening of the American Mind* (New York, NY: Collier Books, Macmillan, 1990), 87.

[14]Mark Van Doren, *Liberal Education* (New York, NY: Henry Holt, 1943, reprint, Boston, MA: Beacon Press, 1959), 63.

[15]Thomas Jefferson, "Report of the Rockfish Gap Commission on the Proposed University of Virginia, 1818," in Hofstadter and Smith, eds., *American Higher Education: A Documentary History*, 1:195. Noah Webster emphasizes the point: "The virtues of men are of more consequence to society than their abilities, and for this reason the heart should be cultivated with more assiduity than the head." "On the Education of Youth in America," in *Essays on Education in the Early Republic*, ed. Frederick Rudolph (Cambridge, MA: Harvard University Press, 1965), 67.

[16]Kimball, *Orators and Philosophers,* xi.

Arnold and Thomas Huxley. Arnold, a Victorian humanist, said we should aim "to know ourselves and the world" by studying "the best that has been thought and said."[17] Huxley, a Darwinian scientist, saw literary works as subjective expressions of emotion, incapable of discerning truth, and proclaimed that "the free employment of reason, in accordance with the scientific method, is the sole method of reaching truth."[18] The gulf between the two exclusivist positions leads to "two cultures," divided by a "gulf of mutual incomprehension—sometimes hostility and dislike, but most of all lack of understanding."[19]

C. *Professional Education v. Liberal Education.* Professional education as it exists today is different from the mechanical, vocational training that Aristotle used to distinguish liberal education. For one thing, responsible professional education is imbued with moral purpose (typically service to humanity) and emphasizes moral means, that is, adherence to a professional code of ethics. This is especially true in Christian circles where "a vocation or calling is a certain kind of life ordained and imposed on man by God for the common good."[20] Furthermore, professional education can be intellectually rigorous and thereby sharpens the critical capacities of its students (for example becoming a doctor, a lawyer, or an engineer is quite rigorous). Therefore, professional education has much in common with many definitions of liberal education. But are they synonymous? If not, what are the differences?

In spite of Aristotle's effort to distinguish liberal education by contrasting it with technical training, many modern educators minimize the distinction by arguing that the dichotomy is "fallacious," "no longer useful," "a gossamer of self-deception" because technical training has

---

[17]Matthew Arnold, "Literature and Science," in *Discourses in America* (London: Macmillan, 1885), 82.

[18]Thomas Huxley, "Science and Culture," in *Science and Education* (New York, NY: Citadel Press, 1964), 135.

[19]C. P. Snow, "The Two Cultures," in *The Two Cultures and the Scientific Revolution* (New York, NY: Cambridge University Press, 1961), 4.

[20]Puritan William Perkins as quoted in Paul Marshall, *A Kind of Life Imposed on Man: Vocation and Social Order from Tyndale to Locke* (Toronto: University of Toronto Press, 1996), 41.

evolved into professional education.[21] It is not uncommon, however, to hear arguments that liberal and professional education are "incommensurably at variance" and that the latter has a "corrupting effect" on higher education.[22] Others are more charitable. Arguing that professional studies are useful, beneficial, even essential ("life could not go on without them"), some observers maintain a distinction between professional studies which "afford scope for the highest and most diversified powers of mind," but for a specific purpose, and those liberal studies which aim at the cultivation of the mind for its own sake.[23] This camp emphasizes that the two "are naturally compatible—but they are emphatically not coincident . . . and both are better served by crisp delimitations."[24]

D. *The Utility and Worth of Liberal Education.* A debate that immediately follows the preceding one questions the utility of a liberal education. Does liberal education serve any useful purpose? What is its utility? Why would a parent spend $100,000 on a liberal education for a son or daughter? Why should a community expend scarce resources ensuring liberal education for succeeding generations? It is quite common to hear parents, even faculty members, say students should get required courses "out of the way" so they can move on to important things, a major that prepares one for a career, a job, a profession. Assuming "education should be useful, whatever your aim in life," students and parents alike label liberal education a necessary evil.[25] They prefer that students focus on what is useful rather than stuffing their heads "with a deal of trash, a great part whereof they usually never . . . think on again

---

[21]Alfred North Whitehead, *The Aims of Education and Other Essays* (New York, NY: Macmillan, 1929), 74; Earl J. McGrath, *Liberal Education in the Professions* (New York, NY: Teachers College, Columbia University, 1959), vi; and Thomas Woody, *Liberal Education for Free Men*, 259.

[22]Thorstein Veblen, *The Higher Learning in America* (New York, NY: Hill and Wang, 1968), 19-20, 23.

[23]John Henry Newman, *The Idea of a University*, ed. Frank M. Turner (London: Longman, Green, 1899; reprint, New Haven, CT: Yale University Press, 1996), 81, 84.

[24]Brann, *Paradoxes of Education in a Republic*, 37-38.

[25]Whitehead, *The Aims of Education and Other Essays*, 2.

as long as they live; and so much of it as does stick by them they are only the worse for."[26]

The other side contends that "knowledge is capable of being its own end."[27] We study theology and Scripture because of a desire to know God, not merely to fill a pulpit; we study astronomy because of curiosity about the nature of the universe, not to be an astronaut; we study politics because we seek justice, not to be a politician. This does not mean that liberal studies are not useful, but that their study emphasizes ends (What is good?) and shuns means (How will I use this?). Liberal education in this form, not surprisingly, turns out to be quite useful for further learning, for oneself, for serving others, and for professional practice. These commentators argue that "a cultivated intellect, because it is a good in itself, brings with it a power and a grace to every work and occupation which . . . enables us to be more useful," as well as better friends, companions, and citizens.[28]

E. ***The Postmodern Challenge.*** Without providing a full-fledged definition of the phenomenon we call postmodernism, we can agree that a central question raised by the postmodern enterprise is whether or not there is objective truth. Some observers insist postmodernism is not the latest phase in the evolution of liberal education but a rejection of the very notion. Others contend that a postmodern liberal education will finally free us from the shackles of ill-founded, oppressive, inherited traditions, ideas, and practices. As such, is postmodernism inherently destructive of liberal education? Is all of education inherently political?

---

[26]John Locke, quoted in Newman, *The Idea of a University*, 113.

[27]Newman argues, "That further advantages accrue to us and redound to others by its possession, over and above what it is in itself, I am very far indeed from denying; but, independent of these, we are satisfying a direct need of our nature in its very acquisition; and, whereas our nature, unlike that of the inferior creation, does not at once reach its perfection, but depends, in order to it, on a number of external aids and appliances, Knowledge, as one of the principal of these, is valuable for what its very presence in us does for us after the manner of a habit, even though it be turned to no further account, nor subserve any direct end." Newman, *The Idea of a University*, 78-79.

[28]Newman, *The Idea of a University*, 119.

Is the pragmatic view of education emerging out of postmodernism capable of sustaining liberal education as a vital pursuit?

The postmodern challenge has the potential to annul and supersede discussions of moral and intellectual virtue, battles between the sciences and the humanities, questions about the worth and utility of liberal education, and efforts to distinguish professional and liberal education. But postmodernism's fate is unpredictable. In the meantime, every campus contends with all five perennial debates.

The Articles

Azusa Pacific University is wrestling with these matters in a very deliberate fashion. We launch our efforts with the publication of this volume. Several faculty members have written original essays in which they offer a perspective on the meaning of liberal education, the effects of contemporary developments, the relationship between professional and liberal education, and the development of a uniquely Christian perspective. The authors do not purport to speak for the institution. These are not authoritative statements, rather they speak to their colleagues in the hope of sparking substantive dialogue about important matters.

Christopher Flannery and Rae Wineland Newstad begin with a philosophic defense of the classical liberal arts tradition. Opening with a graphic depiction of the difference between liberal and technical learning, they argue that the latter is useful but insufficient because technical training can be used for good or ill. By contrast, a liberal education seeks direction on how to use technical training by examining life's important questions, questions of truth, justice, and beauty. Starting with its Socratic origins, the authors trace the development of the liberal arts tradition, show the etymological roots of key terms, review the historical evolution of the liberal arts tradition, and reveal key revolutions within that tradition.

In the second essay, Dennis A. Sheridan outlines contemporary developments that have profoundly shaped today's colleges and universities. Emphasizing the post-Civil War period, he shows how social change—urbanization, immigration, the rise of the middle class, et cetera—altered the character of education by placing new demands upon it. He explains the emergence of professionalism, specialization, pragmatism, postmodernism, and discusses their impact on colleges and universities. Each development has precipitated changes in both the curriculum and the structure of institutions of higher education. Today, we struggle with the effects of those changes.

Phillip V. Lewis and Rosemary Liegler address the relationship between professional and liberal education. Arguing that the historic tension between these two enterprises is unwarranted and unnecessary, they outline commonalties and issue a challenge to collaboration. Professional education, as understood today, has outgrown its merely technical, vocational, and mechanical origins. Liberal education is described as a vital complement to professional education because of its development of intellectual capacities and cultivation of moral purpose. They conclude with a series of recommendations which they hope will lessen tensions between the two camps.

Richard Slimbach offers a personal perspective on how one might re-imagine a Christian liberal arts education. Arguing that re-imagining begins with an assessment of contemporary culture and its influence on students, he proposes a model of liberal education grounded in the present, yet aimed at equipping students to be agents of change throughout their lives. Slimbach's vision requires restructuring the learning environment, revamping disciplinary content, and revising the pedagogical process. He describes a distinctively Christian liberal arts education as celebratory, visionary, communal, interdisciplinary, prophetic, integrative, and redemptive.

Suggested Readings

The provocative perspectives offered by our faculty colleagues in their articles should spark the reader's interest in further study of liberal education. A thorough review of the literature on liberal education would take several lifetimes. We suggest reading selectively in several categories. The opinions and interpretations of the individual authors often conflict, but a wide reading among the following sources will provide an overview.

Some authors and titles are marked in **boldface**; these are reviewed in the second half of this volume.

We recommend reading one or more of several educational classics. These works provide lucid, insightful, and comprehensive accounts unmitigated by secondary interpreters. No one should overlook Plato's *Republic*, especially book VII, where we read about the Socratic vision which prompts the liberal education enterprise. Many other works are worthy of attention including the following: Plato, *Meno*; Aristotle, *Politics* and *Nicomachean Ethics*; Augustine, *On Christian Teaching*; Capella, *Marriage of Philology and Mercury*; Cassiodorus, *Institutiones*; Quintilian, *Training of an Orator*; Erasmus, *The Education of the Christian Prince*; Milton, *Of Education*; John of Salisbury, *Metalogicon*; Mulcaster, *Positions*; More, *Utopia*; Bacon, *New Atlantis*; Rousseau, *Emile*; and Locke, *Some Thoughts Concerning Education.*

The origins of liberal education are found in ancient Greece, and the liberal arts tradition solidified during the Roman era and the Middle Ages. The most frequently cited secondary sources on education during these eras are as follows: Marrou, *A History of Education in Antiquity*; Bonner, *Education in Ancient Rome*; **Wagner, *The Seven Liberal Arts in the Middle Ages***; Abelson, *The Seven Liberal Arts: A Study in Medieval Culture*; and Clarke, *Higher Education in the Ancient World.*

During the Renaissance and early modern period, the classical liberal arts tradition was challenged. The nature of that challenge, and the consequences of it, are sketched in Woodward, *Studies in Education During the Age of the Renaissance, 1400-1600*; Grafton and Jardine, *From Humanism to the Humanities: Education and the Liberal Arts in Fifteenth- and Sixteenth-Century Europe*; Clarke, *Classical Education in Britain, 1500-1900*; and Rothblatt, *Tradition and Change in English Liberal Education.*

The American liberal arts tradition, although less established, is also worthy of careful study. For it is in America we see most presciently the conflation of liberal and professional education, the weaving of the traditional with the progressive, and the growing ambiguity about the meaning of liberal education. For the colonial period, consider Morison, *The Founding of Harvard College*; Pangle and Pangle, *The Learning of Liberty: The Educational Ideas of the American Founders*; Rudolph, *Essays on Education in the Early Republic*; and Cremin, *American Education: The Colonial Experience, 1607-1783*. Broad surveys tracing the contours of liberal education in America include Rudy, *The Evolving Liberal Arts Curriculum*; Schmidt, *The Liberal Arts College: A Chapter in American Cultural History*; Thomas, *The Search for a Common Learning*; and Hofstadter and Smith, *American Higher Education: A Documentary History*.

Many important books on liberal education were published between 1850 and 1950: Van Doren, *Liberal Education*; **Hutchins, *The Higher Learning in America***; Meiklejohn, *The Liberal College;* Whitehead, *The Aims of Education and Other Essays;* and Maritain, *Education at the Crossroads*. It was during this period that the most frequently cited source in this discussion, **Newman, *The Idea of a University*,** was written.

Among books published in the last twenty years, we commend Brann, *Paradoxes of Education in a Republic*; **Bloom, *The Closing of the American Mind***; Oakley, *Community of Learning: The American College and the Liberal Arts Tradition*; **Gaff, *New Life for the College Curriculum*; Kimball, *Orators and Philosophers*; Miller, *The Meaning of General Education*; Boyer** and **Levine, *A Quest for Common Learning;*** Pelikan, *The Idea of the University: A Reexamination*; and Freedman, *Idealism and Liberal Education*. Recent books extolling a pragmatic approach to liberal education include **Kimball, *The Condition of American Liberal Education*; Anderson, *Prescribing the Life of the Mind***; and Orrill, *Education and Democracy: Re-imagining Liberal Learning in America*.

Lastly, there are essays and documents which have profoundly impacted discussion about liberal education such as C. P. Snow's "The Two Cultures," Huxley's "Science and Culture," Arnold's "Literature and Science," and Jefferson's "Rockfish Gap Report." Three influential institutional documents are the Yale Faculty Report of 1828, the **University of Chicago's *The Idea and Practice of General Education***, and **Harvard College's *General Education in a Free Society***. In the last two decades, major reports influencing the discussion about liberal education include *To Reclaim a Legacy: A Report on the Humanities in Higher Education*, *A New Vitality in General Education*, *Strong Foundations*, *50 Hours*, and *The Dissolution of General Education*.

Conclusion

We trust this introduction highlights the contours of the ongoing debate about liberal arts education. It serves no one's purposes to soft-pedal distinctions or inflate differences. But we hope to provoke dialogue about competing and compelling visions. We do our students a disservice when we pick and choose attractive ideas from the shelf, place them in a market basket, and call them a liberal arts education. We may be tempted to simply select Socrates' search for truth, Erasmus' love of classical authors, Locke's passion for liberty, and Dewey's concern for community, each valuable in its own right, but potentially incompatible with one another. Before we make our selections, we should clarify our vision.

We expect that ongoing conversations sparked by this monograph will be fruitful. Still, our idealism is tempered by reality. We tend to agree with Mark Van Doren who wrote "Liberal education can never be quite perfect, since it is ideal; but at any given time it is good in proportion to the clarity with which it is conceived and the effort which that clarity inspires."[29]

---

[29]Van Doren, *Liberal Education*, preface to Beacon Press reprint.

Part One

ഇ൱

The Articles

The Classical Liberal Arts Tradition

by Christopher Flannery and Rae Wineland Newstad

Presidents, governors, educators, and other civic leaders have spoken frequently and passionately in recent years about various crises of American education. Among those most often emphasized is the need for a highly skilled workforce in this technologically progressive world. And there is such a need. Foremost in the minds of many college students at the time of graduation is getting a job. This is altogether fitting and proper: A sound education should give students greater career opportunities and prepare them to make a significant contribution in their chosen field. One should add that the ability to earn a decent living—to have the self sufficiency and the independence that come with that—is a great foundation of individual liberty, moral responsibility, and self-government.

CHRISTOPHER FLANNERY is professor of political science and chair of the Department of History and Political Science at Azusa Pacific University. He is a graduate of California State University, Northridge (B.A.), The London School of Economics and Political Science, University of London (M.A.), and Claremont Graduate School (M.A., Ph.D.). **RAE WINELAND NEWSTAD** is an assistant professor of history in the College of Liberal Arts and Sciences at Azusa Pacific University. She is a graduate of Colorado State University (B.A.), University of Colorado at Boulder (M.A.), and University of Oklahoma (Ph.D.).

Technical training and liberal education, however, are two very distinct things, and institutions of higher learning do not exist primarily for the former but for the latter. The reasons for this are not always as apparent to the student as they might be. Indeed, they are not always as apparent as they should be to institutions of higher learning. What is the distinction between technical training and liberal education, and why is it essential for institutions of higher learning to make this distinction?[1]

A passage in Martin Gilbert's monumental biography of Winston Churchill suggests an answer to these questions. There we are reminded of a grim episode in modern history that we forget at our peril. Just fifty-five years ago, in the autumn of 1942, information was smuggled out of Nazi Germany through neutral Switzerland revealing to the outside world "the extent of the German slaughter of Jews on the eastern front, the murder by gas of Polish Jews in three special 'death' camps at Chelmno, Belzec, and Treblinka, and of the deportation of Jews from France, Belgium, and Holland to an 'unknown destination' in the East."[2]

It was only two years later that this "unknown destination" was identified as Auschwitz, where Jews were being gassed at the rate of about 12,000 men, women, and children a day. As Churchill wrote at the time, this was "probably the greatest and most horrible crime ever committed in the whole history of the world, and it has been done by scientific machinery by nominally civilized men."[3] The German people were the most technically advanced—one might say the most highly educated—people in the world at that time. Doctors, nurses, psychologists, educators, scientists, engineers, accountants, lawyers, and the whole array of other highly skilled and "nominally civilized" men and women, were devoting their considerable skills, acquired at great effort and expense, to the extermination of a people.

Our century, the most technologically advanced in history, with more technically skilled people per square mile than could once have been imagined, stands out as a century in which genocide is a term with which every grade school child must become familiar. As communism takes its uncertain and much awaited departure from the world, let us not forget

---

[1]Some of the following reflections are adapted from an address to the Senior Convocation at Azusa Pacific University in 1992.

[2]Martin Gilbert, *Winston S. Churchill: The Road to Victory, 1941-1945*, vol. VII (Boston, MA: Houghton Mifflin, 1986), 245.

[3]Ibid., 847.

the Bolshevik extermination of the Kulaks, the millions sacrificed to China's political experiments, and of course the killing fields in Cambodia—all in the name of scientific socialism and progress, but in fact amounting to a new phenomenon in the world: scientific savagery. More generally, if less dramatically, human beings throughout history have proven as apt to use their acquired skills to take advantage of one another as to confer benefits on one another.

What does this tell us about education and about the relation between liberal education on the one hand and the acquisition of technical skill—job training—on the other? It points to the heart of the matter. Every art, craft, or technical skill (what the ancient Greeks called *techne*) may be used in the service of justice or injustice, good or evil. It may be used to dignify our humanity or to degrade it.[4] For this reason, the central and most urgent question of education becomes, What is good? And the most urgent practical question becomes, How do we learn to do what is good and avoid what is evil?

These, of course, were the kinds of questions posed by Socrates to the ancient Athenians, who did so much to give meaning to our word "technology." And for doing them this service, they gave him the hemlock. Nonetheless, in his death Socrates proved victorious over his judges, as he predicted he would. His life became the source of the idea of liberal education in the West. His questions became central to the liberal arts curriculum as it developed through the Middle Ages and into the modern era. They are the human questions, and they animated the study of what came to be called the "humanities."

These questions reflect the ultimate human need—to know the source and reason of all goodness. Because of this elemental need, as Plato's Socrates would put it, every education is radically—decisively—deficient or incomplete to the extent that it is not informed or illuminated by "the greatest study," the study of that "for the sake of which" we do all that we do.[5] The "human questions" arise from human nature itself. "Man by nature desires to know," as Aristotle wrote.[6] And what "man by

---

[4]As Socrates points out to Polemarchus in Plato's *Republic*, the medical art is equally able to guard against disease and to produce it. Plato, *The Republic of Plato*, trans. Allan Bloom (New York, NY: Basic Books, 1991), 332d-333e.

[5]Plato, *The Republic of Plato*, 505a2, 505d7-8.

[6]Aristotle, *Metaphysics*, trans. W. D. Ross (http://classics.mit.edu/Aristotle/metaphysics.1.i.html), first line.

nature" ultimately most needs to know is the final end, or highest good, or that for the sake of which all things exist.[7] The Christian heirs to the classical tradition gave their own distinctive expression to the ultimate human need toward which all profitable human inquiry is directed: It is the need to know God.[8]

The consequence of forgetting this need and the world of questions arising from it, of treating these questions as answered by race, class, history, or culture, or of replacing them with the acquisition of technical competence or job training, is brutally clear. It is to risk producing computer programmers, scientists, business managers, doctors, and lawyers who are at best technocratic barbarians. It is to place in the hands of succeeding generations ever greater power over their world and their fellow human beings, and to fail to teach them the ends to which this awesome power is to be used.

However much America—and the world—needs technically skilled workers and professionals, there can be no doubt of the critically greater need for liberally educated citizens and human beings who can distinguish good from evil, justice from injustice, what is noble and beautiful from what is base and degrading. Such men and women will be fit to enjoy and confer on one another all the blessings of life that are within our power. Not just in the workplace, but in the home and the neighborhood, in the public square, the town meeting, and the church. And not just as technically skilled professionals (with, one trusts, highly competitive salaries) but as sons and daughters, parents, friends, and fellow citizens, and as children of God.

Pillars of Wisdom

Liberal education is commonly associated with education in the liberal arts. What are the liberal arts? What is the relation of the liberal arts disciplines to one another? These basic if not simple questions are, in effect, already answered by every Christian institution of higher learning

---

[7]Aristotle, *Nicomachean Ethics*, trans. Martin Ostwald (Englewood Cliffs, NJ: Prentice Hall, 1962), 1094a1-26, 1177a12-1178a8.

[8]Thomas Aquinas, *Summa Theologica*, Question 94, Second Article, Objection 3 (http://www.knight.org/advent/summa/209402.htm).

that includes among its avowed purposes education in the liberal arts, or liberal education. That these questions have been answered, however—in mission statements, institutional structures, and curricula—does not necessarily mean that they are being asked. Colleges and universities like other institutions perpetuate themselves in part by taking certain things for granted. Among the things necessarily taken for granted are sometimes the most important things, including the central purposes of the institution itself. At the most established institutions, these purposes are most deeply embedded in tradition.

Our contemporary understandings have arisen in self-conscious response to a particular twenty-five hundred year tradition or history of the liberal arts. What then, speaking historically, is the tradition of the liberal arts? As we have said, the liberal arts tradition has its origin in the classical thought of ancient Greece. The tradition originates in response to the most needful questions, arising from human nature, and posed by incipient philosophy—What is being? What is wisdom? What is virtue? What is good?

An unprecedented search for truth accessible to reason about the whole of things led necessarily to the search for truth about the place of humanity within this whole.[9] This revolutionary endeavor of the human mind—rightly associated above all with the names of Socrates, Plato, and Aristotle—gave rise to a structured and systematic body of reflection. After Greek philosophy had reached full flower in the fourth century B.C., scholars and teachers sought to establish a curriculum to prepare students for the higher and more difficult studies. Out of these efforts came what was called the *enkuklios paideia*, the learning circle, from which we get our word encyclopedia.[10]

A first century B.C. scholar and statesman named Marcus Terentius Varro codified this slowly developing curriculum into nine disciplines and introduced it to Rome. His work provided a model for Latin scholars

---

[9]Socrates describes the historic turn in his own relentless search for the truth in *Phaedo*, 96a-100.

[10]The Academy founded by Plato—a leading center, to say the least, of liberal education—endured for nine hundred years. It had some difficulty preserving and perpetuating in their full breadth and depth the teachings of its founder, as have American universities and colleges with far less to live up to. What brought the Academy to an end was an edict of the emperor Justinian in 529 A.D. as part of an effort to impose religious conformity throughout the Roman empire.

("encyclopedists") of the later Roman period; such famous thinkers as St. Augustine, Boethius, and Cassiodorus refined and developed the tradition; and by the fifth to sixth century A.D., a canon of seven liberal arts (dropping Varro's architecture and medicine) had been established and incorporated into Christian education.

These seven arts were divided into the two familiar categories: the trivium, consisting of the verbal arts of logic, grammar, and rhetoric; and the quadrivium, consisting of the numerical arts of mathematics, geometry, music, and astronomy. These disciplines came to constitute the liberal arts, which "provided the basic content and form of intellectual life [in Europe] for several centuries." The liberal arts were, in effect, regarded as "the seven pillars of wisdom."[11]

The Hierarchy of Disciplines

How, in this tradition, are the liberal arts related to one another, to education as a whole, and to Christian education? The trivium and quadrivium mean literally "the three ways" and "the four ways." These disciplines are, as Thomas Aquinas said, ways or "paths preparing the mind for the other philosophic disciplines."[12] The liberal arts are basic; they are the foundation of a full liberal education, which rises from them and reaches beyond them.

There is a distinctive mode of reasoning appropriate to the different disciplines. As Aristotle noted, an educated person does "not look for precision in all things alike, but in each class of things such precision as accords with the subject-matter, and so much as is appropriate to the inquiry."[13] The carpenter and the geometer investigate the right angle in different ways. One should not demand mathematical precision of a statesman defending the cause of justice, nor should one accept enthymemes from a mathematician demonstrating the Pythagorean theorem. Yet both mathematical and moral or political discourse reveal elements of the truth about the world in which we live.

---

[11]David L. Wagner, ed., *The Seven Liberal Arts in the Middle Ages* (Bloomington, IN: Indiana University Press, 1983), 1, 256; see especially 1-57, 248-272 for general treatments of the development of the liberal arts tradition.

[12]Ibid., 251.

[13]Aristotle, *Nicomachean Ethics*, 1098a26-28.

There is an inherent hierarchy within the liberal arts themselves and in the whole educational edifice of which they are the foundation. According to the tradition, a student should first acquire a facility with language/logic because this discipline is necessary for all other studies. (For the liberal arts, as elsewhere, "In the beginning is the word.") Youth is also traditionally held to be capable of acquiring the art of mathematics because it is abstract, whereas certain other disciplines require experience to be understood. The practical disciplines of ethics and politics, for example, depend upon the accumulation of experience and, most important, the development of the capacity to subject one's passions and appetites to reason.

Last comes the highest and most difficult study, the study of first causes. For the pagan Greeks and Romans, this study culminated in metaphysics. With the assimilation of the pagan tradition to Christianity, the highest study became, of course, theology, the divine science. And the liberal arts were throughout Christendom, from the time of Augustine to that of Aquinas and well after, understood as the necessary preparation for the understanding of Scripture. The highest purpose of the liberal arts in the Christian tradition is to prepare students for the lofty and rigorous discipline of understanding in its fullness "the truth [that] shall make you free" (John 8:32).

The Unifying Principle

Within the historical development of the liberal arts themselves, the question is continuously raised of the meaning, purpose, and unifying principle of the liberal arts. For two thousand years, the nature of this question remains in a decisive respect the same. In the sixteenth and seventeenth centuries, a radical reorientation or disorientation occurs, a revolution in thought marking a departure from the previous two millennia and inaugurating the modern era. It is impossible to understand the significance of this modern revolution, however, without fully understanding the still living—if battle-scarred—tradition it was intended to replace.

In this tradition, the liberal arts, the *artes liberales*, are literally arts of freedom. Traditionally this meant, among other things, the arts of free men as opposed to slaves. Slaves are subjected to the will of others, mere tools or instruments of alien purposes, unable to choose for themselves.

People are subjected to slavery by conquest. To prevent such conquest, to preserve that freedom which is a condition for the exercise of the liberal arts, requires other arts, arts of necessity, most notably the art of war. Other necessities also encroach upon our freedom and our very survival—the needs for food, shelter, and clothing, for example. Arts are developed to secure the necessary material conditions for existence. Economics (from the Greek *oikonomike*, household management) is the name given to the general art of acquiring such necessary material goods. The successful cultivation of the arts of necessity seems to be a condition for the flourishing of the arts of freedom.

Unlike the compulsory arts of war and economics, the liberal arts are not forced upon us by the needs of mere life but are chosen for the sake of a good life. They are arts not for the acquisition or accomplishment of necessary things but for the use of choice-worthy things. They were distinguished traditionally, for this reason, from the manual or mechanical arts as well. That is, they are not merely instrumental arts but arts that are in some respect an end in themselves. They are arts to be exercised, as it were, after the battles are fought and won, the fields are plowed, and the buying and selling are done. They are, as Aristotle would say, the "leisure" arts.[14] Our students are (perhaps painfully) amused around exam time when we remind them that our words "school," "scholar," and "scholarship" are derived from the Greek word "*schole*," which means leisure—and that "schools" are places where "scholars" learn to make the best use of their "*schole*"!

Our young scholars know only too well that school involves toil, not to say drudgery. Where is the *schole* for our scholars? Where is the *libertas* for our liberal artists? The idea of the liberal arts involves a tension—inherent in human nature itself—between freedom and ruling purpose. An art is a skill (*techne*). What is done with art is distinguished from what occurs by chance or by nature. Arts do not grow like the grass in the fields. Human purpose, design, and conscious method infuse the arts. Rigor and precision are involved in acquiring and in exercising every art. It is not by chance that the various liberal arts are traditionally called "disciplines." This suggests to us that leisure properly speaking is

---

[14]Aristotle, *Politics*, trans. H. Rackham (http://hydra.perseus.tufts.edu/cgi-bin/text?lookup=aristot.+pol.+1337b27#anch1337b,2), 1337b27-1337b42, 1333b37-1334a34. It is worth reflecting on what Aristotle means when he says that leisure is "the first principle" (the *arche*, the beginning and end) of all activity.

not mere idleness and that freedom is not random meandering or arbitrary willfulness. The liberal arts are, paradoxically, the leisure disciplines, the disciplines of freedom. They are arts not only of freedom but for freedom. They prepare us to deserve, by using well, "the blessings of liberty."

The liberal arts have to do with that element of our being in which our freedom most essentially resides—namely, our mind or spirit—as opposed to what is subject to physical compulsion, our bodies. This is why medicine, for example, came to be excluded from the canon. One might say that the first principle or axiom of the liberal arts is—in the words of Thomas Jefferson—that "Almighty God hath created the mind free."[15] And the first task of the liberal arts is to secure the liberation of the mind from those many fetters that can bind it: notably ignorance, prejudice, and the influence of the passions. In and through this essential freedom, the freedom of the mind, our "humanity" is revealed. The integrative principle of the liberal arts is this idea, *humanitas*, which gives us our word for the humanities.

This unifying idea was expressed for two thousand years in the form of a vital question, the central animating question of the liberal arts tradition—asked alike by classical rationalists, Roman Catholics, Renaissance humanists, and Protestant Christians. In the words of the Westminster Larger Catechism, words that would be as familiar and understandable to Aristotle in the fourth century B.C. and Thomas Aquinas in the thirteenth century A.D. as they were to Protestant communicants in the seventeenth century: "What is the chief and highest end of man?"[16]

The Revolution of Modernity

Even as late as the seventeenth century, the ancient tradition of the liberal arts was still intact—though certainly under siege. Thomas Hobbes could still write in 1640 that it was Aristotle, "whose opinions are at this day, and in these parts of greater authority than any other human

---

[15]Thomas Jefferson, "A Bill for Establishing Religious Freedom," *Writings* (New York, NY: Literary Classics of the United States, 1984), 346.

[16]Westminster Larger Catechism, (http://www.reformed.org/documents/larger1.html).

writings."[17] And the essential idea of Aristotle against which Hobbes and other founders of the modern world would rebel was an idea that had been fully adopted by both Roman Catholic and Protestant Christianity, an idea which, in a sense, was the animating idea of Western civilization itself—the idea of the final end or highest good toward which all human endeavor should be directed. As Hobbes wrote,

> There is no such *finis ultimus*, utmost aim, nor *summum bonum*, greatest good, as is spoken of in the books of the old moral philosophers. . . . Felicity is a continual progress of the desire, from one object to another; the attaining of the former, being still but the way to the latter. . . . So that in the first place, I put for a general inclination of all mankind, a perpetual and restless desire of power after power, that ceaseth only in death.[18]

The rejection of the idea of a final end or highest good as the central concern of life and education marks a decisive break in the two thousand year tradition of the liberal arts. With this break, the arts of freedom begin to be replaced by the arts of (mere) necessity. Education oriented to the highest good is replaced by education in the service of the lowest common denominator—avoidance of death or preservation of life and physical comfort. Mastery of nature for "the relief of man's estate" begins to become the governing objective of all education. The highest aim of education becomes the aim of a distinctively modern science in which "knowledge and human power are synonymous." This aim is to "enlarge the power and empire of mankind in general over the universe."[19]

Modern thought is characterized by a wholesale rejection of the most fundamental premises of both Christianity and classical learning, and therefore of the liberal arts tradition that to a large degree brought Athens and Jerusalem together in Rome. From at least the time of Thomas Hobbes, our most influential thinkers have in a variety of forms rejected both revelation and reason, have denied both God and the freedom of the mind with which God had been held to have endowed human beings.

---

[17]Thomas Hobbes, *The Elements of Law Natural and Politic* (1640), online, (http://socserv2.socsci.mcmaster.ca/~econ/ugcm/3113/hobbes/elelaw), I, ch. 17, sec. 1.

[18]Thomas Hobbes, *Leviathan or the Matter, Forme and Power of a Commonwealth Ecclesiasticall and Civil* (Oxford: Basil Blackwell, 1960), 63-64.

[19]Francis Bacon, *Novum Organum*, I. 3; I. 129, in *Advancement of Learning and Novum Organum* (New York, NY: Willey, 1900), 315, 366.

Historical Diversity

Thus far, we have soared over whole epochs in an instant, ignoring worlds of confusion, disputation, and multitudinous variety—without, we trust, distorting the essential truth too much. There is, however, perhaps some consolation in recalling that the liberal arts developed and reached their current state with frequent and profound uncertainty interwoven with the greatest cultural and political epochs of Western civilization. Reflection on this historical diversity can teach us moderation in the midst of our contemporary "culture wars."

The great minds of Greek antiquity retained their power to inspire and enlighten throughout even Europe's darkest centuries. The intellectual history of the western Middle Ages reveals an inexorable, albeit sometimes painful, reabsorption of the Greek heritage. The outlines of the Greek reconquest were plain to see in the twelfth and thirteenth centuries' "medieval renaissance," founded, as it was, largely upon the West's rediscovery of Aristotle and upon the monumental intellectual labors of Thomas Aquinas, who sought to do nothing less than to reconcile reason with revelation. The result was the great, uneasy synthesis that came to characterize the High Middle Ages, a synthesis between what Matthew Arnold called Hebraism and Hellenism, the "two points of influence," he declared, between which our world moves.[20]

Medieval universities, agents for the dissemination of the new learning, literally "sprouted" all over Europe during and after the twelfth century; many, such as the University of Paris, originated as cathedral or monastic schools.[21] The University of Paris, a model for succeeding establishments throughout the Western world, acquired its charter in 1200 A.D. from the realm's secular monarch, Philip Augustus, and subsequent acknowledgment (in 1231 A.D.) from the pope, who intended to make Paris the leading theological academy not only in France but in all of Western Europe. Notwithstanding, Oxford University rivaled Paris and in the next century surpassed it as the center of European scholarship. At Oxford, languages, mathematics, and the natural sciences outshone

---

[20]In part, the Middle Ages are defined by the profound interaction, not only of Christianity, but of Judaism and Islam, with classical rationalism.

[21]Stanley James Curtis, *History of Education in Great Britain* (Westport, CT: Greenwood Press, [1953] 1971), 56-57.

theological pursuits, earning Roger Bacon's praise as the only western institution where one could find the complete teaching of "mathematical sciences."[22]

In every new university, the tensions between the two "modes of wisdom," Christian and pagan, found expression.[23] With the official sanction of the papacy after 1263 A.D., Aristotle emerged as dominant in almost every academic field: politics, physics, aesthetics, metaphysical philosophy, biology, astronomy, law. "Aristotle becomes the foundation of the curriculum in the Faculty of Arts."[24] Aristotle represented the "reason" of the "reason and faith" formula: Thomas Aquinas had argued that the Church need not fear reason, for "reason and faith" would prove ultimately compatible. As the Thomistic synthesis petrified into the rigid formalities of scholasticism, both faith and reason fell increasingly into question.

Old Wine: New Bottles

Scholasticism's brittle forms shattered under the relentless blows delivered by men like William of Ockham. By the mid-fourteenth century, the medieval intellectual world of the schoolmen had receded and the definitions of the modern age, marked by skepticism, secularism, and science, began to take shape.

Guided by the humanists of the fifteenth and sixteenth centuries, higher education incorporated more of the "human letters" (classical Greek and Roman literature) and less theological (medieval scholastic) content.[25] In that age of powerful, ambitious new national monarchies and the concomitant development of cultural nationalism, a liberal education was expected to mold an individual's character with the greater goal of building a responsible "civilized" citizen.[26]

---

[22]Ibid., 68-69.

[23]T. L. Jarman, *Landmarks in the History of Education: English Education as Part of the European Tradition* (London: Cresset Press, 1951), 103-105.

[24]Curtis, *History of Education in Great Britain*, 66-67; and Jarman, *Landmarks*, 105. Jarman claims that "the influence of Aristotle on medieval thought and higher study can scarcely be exaggerated." *Landmarks*, 104.

[25]Patricia Beesley, *The Revival of the Humanities in American Education* (New York, NY: Columbia University Press, 1940), 29.

[26]R. R. Bolgar, *The Classical Heritage and Its Beneficiaries* (Cambridge: Cambridge University Press, 1954), 382-383.

Toward that end, the humanists struggled to revivify the classical age through imitation, often slavish imitation, of both classical language and culture, training in the process both mind and body. The schoolmen, having grown accustomed to positions of prominence in the academic field, and seeing their methods, assumptions, and reputations threatened, fought back. The strife was often bitter, as the schoolmen defended claims of harmony and unity of the Christian and pagan worldviews.

As this battle continued, scholasticism's "unimaginative intellectualism" provoked unremitting and frequently satirical criticism from proponents of the "new learning." The emerging commercial middle class was accruing more and more wealth by dint of the merchants' faith in progress, individual effort, self-reliance, and hard work. To these industrious elements, the whole "ethos" of the institutional Church seemed hopelessly arid and anachronistic, including, or more properly beginning with, an educational establishment long in the grip of scholasticism.

In the mid-fifteenth century, one of the last (and the most inflexible) defenders of rigid scholasticism, Bishop Reginald Pecock, pined away almost unlamented in an English prison (hated perhaps as much for his personal vanity as for his die-hard support of scholasticism). By this time, "intelligent men" had grown to "despise the scholars of the old learning as obscurantist logic-choppers, and the prestige of the Church supported by these scholars suffered, too."[27]

Humanism's "new learning" emphasized the study of Latin, Greek, and to a lesser degree Hebrew, appealing directly to the classics and early Fathers rather than to their medieval interpreters. A new generation of scholars (still mostly clerics, to be sure) brought a sharply critical method to the study of theology. They were paving the way not only for a return to primitive Christianity but for a full-scale repudiation, in the process, of extra-biblical medieval accretions: papal presumption, superstition, and inevitably the scholasticism so closely identified with them.

Subjects other than theology attracted the humanist scholar even more intensely: mathematics, history, medicine, and civil (not canon) law. Yet while anti-Christian bias was present in the humanism of the fourteenth and fifteenth centuries, one must be careful not to overstress its

---

[27]A. R. Myers, *England in the Late Middle Ages*, 8th ed. (Middlesex, England: Penguin Books, 1971), 169.

prominence. The influence of the institutional Church still permeated all western life, from the castle to the hut, including all teaching, whether dispensed at the renowned universities or in the modest parish classroom. To be an atheist (and proclaim it) was almost inconceivable. Even the vigorous new secular states displayed a reluctance to defy outright the claims of the Church Universal. Furthermore, as creatures of the Middle Ages, the universities long retained the forms and curricular patterns established at their founding, blunting much of the impact of new ideas. In the sixteenth century, the old trivium and quadrivium survived; newer subjects when adopted enhanced the older curriculum but did not replace it.[28]

Rebirth and Reform

In the sixteenth century, two "movements of the mind" assaulted the spiritual and social unity of earlier centuries. With the coincident phenomena of Renaissance and Reformation came new, albeit divergent, views of education, its goals, its content, its means of transmission. Contrary to expectations both then and now, however, the changes admitted into university curricula appear minor, given the magnitude of the intellectual forces at work in the sixteenth century. In fact, the purposes of a "liberal education" can be said to have been enlarged: whereas Latin was primarily studied in the Middle Ages preparatory to a clerical vocation, Greek and other classical studies after the 1500s were frequently pursued not for their vocational utility, "but rather [as] a training of the mind, and more particularly the mind of a gentleman."[29]

The life of Erasmus of Rotterdam can legitimately be said to have typified the ideal of Renaissance humanism. The Renaissance in general was decidedly unorthodox (although rarely anti-sacerdotal, at least not scandalously so) in approach; Erasmus proffered an individualized version of the Old Faith. While he did not consciously abandon Catholicism but rather poked fun at its foibles, his critics certainly saw where such acerbic commentaries as his *Colloquies* could lead. In 1526, for example, the

---

[28]Martin L. Clark, *Classical Education in Britain, 1500-1900* (Cambridge: Cambridge University Press, 1959), 21.

[29]Jarman, *Landmarks*, 137.

theological faculty at the University of Paris attacked Erasmus' work as heretical and their author as pagan.[30] In fact, like other humanists of the day, Erasmus did elevate pagan literature to the level of Scripture in authority, inviting the wrath of his contemporary, and sometime correspondent, Martin Luther.

Like Erasmus, Luther and other reformers valued the study and comprehension of letters, especially Hebrew, Greek, and Latin, but their interest was not in revitalizing the classics as a means by which pagan civilization could be absorbed and imitated. Rather, suspicious of the secularists' veneration of pagan culture, the reformers prized the study of languages as a means by which to study Scripture and restore the simplicity and authenticity of early Christian worship. In Protestant states, the reformers remodeled old institutions and founded new ones (the first Protestant university opened at Marburg in 1527). Individually, the reformers praised and participated in higher studies. Philip Melanchthon, for instance, penned Latin and Greek grammars as well as textbooks for theology, rhetoric, and logic.[31]

Although the content necessarily changed, reformed universities maintained the older established framework. More pronounced change, however, is evident in the reformers insistence on and practical encouragement of elementary and secondary education. The doctrine of the priesthood of all believers inevitably entailed the education of the population, both males and females, to prepare them to read and interpret Scripture for themselves, and to do so in their own language. In 1559, school regulations for Wurttemberg, to cite one example, stipulated the establishment of specifically "German schools" in villages and small towns, offering free instruction to the ordinary citizens in such subjects as German language, religion, and music. Lutheran authorities supervised the licensing and operation of these schools.[32]

English, Swiss, and Scottish reformers followed suit in broadening opportunities for education and emphasizing use of the vernacular, especially at the elementary and secondary levels. In England, reformers

---

[30]Erasmus, *Ten Colloquies*, trans. Craig R. Thompson (Indianapolis, IN: Bobbs-Merrill, 1957), xxvi-xxvii.

[31]Jarman, *Landmarks*, 148-149.

[32]Ibid., pp. 150-151, 154-155. Other textbooks published by reformers include *The Christian Education of Boys* by Ulrich Zwingli (1523), and *First Book of Discipline* by John Knox (1560).

not only translated the Bible itself, but wrote other spiritual works in English. Evidently, literacy was widespread enough to warrant this innovation, and the printing press gave access to the printed word to all but the very poorest in the population.[33]

The other side in the great religious struggle of the sixteenth century, the forces of the counter-reformation, fully recognized the use of education in their fight to halt and turn back the Protestant tide. Shortly after its creation, the Jesuit order devoted much of its energies to the teaching mission. From Portugal to Prague, Jesuit universities opened. They accorded Latin pre-eminence as the tool of communication; at the university level, three years of philosophy (Aristotelian and Thomist) were followed by four years of theology. Within these broadly defined courses was instruction in mathematics, law, medicine, and other sciences. The Jesuit institutions admitted both clerical and lay students.[34]

Enlightenment

The seventeenth century witnessed unprecedented expansion by Europe's powerful new nation-states. Worldwide discoveries of heretofore unexplored lands led in turn to growth of commerce and the need for supporting studies: improved science, accounting, mathematics, and navigation. The educational establishments of previous centuries appeared increasingly out-of-touch, and their course offerings less and less relevant to the modern age. Early in the century, profound disgust was shown in England toward "the 'gerund-grinding' of the grammar schools."[35] Support grew, especially among the up-and-coming commercial middle class, for practical subjects taught in English, which would provide the required expertise to sustain and expand the nation's business success. Thinkers like Francis Bacon and John Milton attacked traditional education for its stilted formalism and hostility to change: in Bacon's words, "the sciences we now possess are merely systems for the nice ordering and setting forth of things already invented; not methods of invention or

---

[33]Curtis, *History of Education in Great Britain*, 102.
[34]Jarman, *Landmarks*, 156-159.
[35]Curtis, *History of Education in Great Britain*, 110.

directions for new works."[36] John Locke too expressed only contempt for the weaknesses of traditional education: "when a man's head is stuffed with [it], he has got the just furniture of a pedant."[37] While the trenchant critiques produced by Locke and others had minimal effect on the older schools, they did their part in driving the more apt students away from the old institutions and into the modern private academies which more effectively served the needs of the middle class.

In the age of scientific revolution, practical learning attracted the most progressive elements of society. According to Campbell's *London Tradesman* (1747), a student might expend seven years attaining at best, "a partial Knowledge of the Classics" and still know only "trifles of no Signification to his future Happiness." The "misfortune of the Public Schools" was revealed in the fact that that same student and his colleagues, exposed at least to Greek and Latin, "know no more of their Mother Tongue (except the mere sound) than if they had been born in *Japan*, or at the *Cape of Good Hope*."[38] Demands for a utilitarian education, scientifically based and taught in the vernacular, grew ever more insistent. Again, while the universities of Oxford, Cambridge, Paris, and elsewhere effectively ignored the calls for reform, private academies in England and newly funded universities in the German states filled the need.

The Enlightenment's revolutionary mystique can easily conceal the fact that some of that age's most radical thinkers received their training at the continent's most rigidly traditional institutions. In Catholic Europe, the Jesuits retained (until 1773, when to the great satisfaction of their enemies, the Order was temporarily disbanded) a near-monopoly on education, yet among their most famous graduates one can number some of their most intransigent foes: Condorcet, Helvetius, Malesherbes, Diderot and the Jesuits' and the established Church's *bete noir*, Voltaire. The militant Order had come under fire from many directions (moral, political, theological); the *philosophes* and other "progressive" elements, especially in France, found fault in particular with the Jesuit academic

---

[36]Francis Bacon, *First Book of Aphorisms*, in *The Age of Reason: The 17th Century Philosophers*, selected and introduced by Stuart Hampshire (New York, NY: Mentor Books, 1956), 24.

[37]Quoted in Curtis, *History of Education in Great Britain*, 115.

[38]R. Campbell, *The London Tradesman* [London: 1747], in *European Society in the Eighteenth Century: Documentary History of Western Civilization*, eds. Robert and Elborg Forster (New York, NY: Harper Row, 1969), 303-304.

role. The Jesuits' interpretation of rhetoric and the classics brought charges of obscurantism. What the schools needed, their opponents claimed, was more science, contemporary history, and modern languages, all taught of course by non-clerics.

As elitists, however, the *philosophes* could not heartily support discarding the classics *in toto* (among other things, they loved their classical education and the sense of superiority it afforded them). They would be satisfied in reality with the desacrilization and bifurcation of learning: teaching should be removed forcibly from the grasp of the Orders and put into the hands of more "congenial elements." The content of the teaching could then reflect the pupils' class and vocational requirements. A classical education, with full opportunity to study the latest science, should be reserved for the elites. If there were any value at all in bothering to educate the *peuple* (and this was by no means certain), vocational or technical training better suited them.

Democratic Vistas

With the spread of democracy in the nineteenth century, elitism of this rigid variety became harder and harder to defend. Education had to accompany the franchise down the social ladder. The question was no longer *whether* to educate the lower classes, but *how*. The modernist demanded new curricula: practical, utilitarian, scientific. Typical of the fierce debates between traditional classicists and their reform-minded opponents is the highly publicized editorial position of the *Edinburgh Review* countered ably by Edward Copleston, Fellow of Oriel.

The *Edinburgh Review*, which had begun an exposé of English education with attacks on the Public Schools, turned its attention in the first decade of the nineteenth century to Oxford. Calling the ascendancy of classical education "preposterous," the journal attacked curricula at the universities in general and Oxford in particular as outmoded, useless, and "utterly absurd."[39] How, it queried, could classical studies be defended on the basis of utilitarianism?

---

[39]Curtis, *History of Education in Great Britain*, 115.

Copleston's reply, according to S. J. Curtis, "constitutes one of the noblest vindications of literary studies, and of classical literature in particular, that has ever been penned." In Copleston's own words, recorded [originally anonymously] in his *Reply to the Calumnies of the Edinburgh Review against Oxford*,

> In the cultivation of literature is found that common link, which, among the higher and middle departments of life, unites the jarring sects and sub-divisions in one interest, which supplies common topics, and kindles common feelings, unmixed with those narrow prejudices with which all professions are more or less infected. The knowledge too, which is thus acquired, expands and enlarges the mind, excites its faculties, and . . . thus, without directly qualifying a man for any of the employments of life, it enriches and ennobles all.[40]

Despite this and other such spirited defenses of traditional learning in England and elsewhere, changing social, economic, and political conditions throughout the West transformed education. German schools specializing in practical studies—or "knowledge of the *realia* of life"—were commonly called burgher schools (*Realschulen*) in contrast to the *Gymnasia* or humanist institutions. The state governments involved themselves deeply in educational issues; successful monarchs required both skilled administrators and capable merchants. Therefore, reforms after the Enlightenment tended to favor practical curricula (Humboldt's advocacy of "general education" at all levels notwithstanding) as well as secular instruction.[41]

Nevertheless, well into the modern era, European education mirrored society's class divisions. Noble sons in the German states, for example, retained exclusive access to certain elite academies while enjoying segregated facilities and private tutors at the universities which, in Holborn's words, "were institutes for the development of the intellect exclusively." Catering only to graduates of the *Gymnasia*, the traditional German university supplied a liberal arts education of which philosophy was foundational to every department. Germany lagged in its teaching of

---

[40]Ibid., 433.

[41]Hajo Holborn, *A History of Modern Germany: 1648-1840* (New York, NY: Knopf, 1968), 472-475.

and contributions to the fields of the natural sciences, being closer to France than to England in its attitudes toward these pursuits.[42]

By no means was a modern curriculum easily instituted even in England, the home of the industrial revolution and Benthamite utilitarianism. The nineteenth century witnessed a ferocious struggle for the recognition of science in a nation where "classical tradition held sway" in "the official educational system." Such reform as did succeed "took place chiefly outside the established universities and sometimes in spite of their opposition."[43] One new institution, the University of London, rose on the sixteenth-century foundation laid by merchant Thomas Gresham. In 1575 Gresham had endowed a London college with a mansion and seven professorships—medicine, geometry, civil law, rhetoric, divinity, astronomy, and music. A center for the training of Nonconformists and other middle-class dissenters, the college attained the status and degree-granting power, after prolonged opposition by both Oxford and Cambridge, only in 1836. Its purely secular character inspired Thomas Arnold and others to refer to the new University of London as "that godless institution in Gower Street."[44]

After 1850, popular education, even more expressly vocational and technical in nature, appeared in England. Both primary education and adult learning spread. Curricula focused on modern, non-classical offerings: reading, writing, arithmetic, bookkeeping, geography, and natural sciences. Among the nineteenth-century establishments aimed at England's adult working-class population, the network of Mechanics' Institutes was surely the most extensive and influential. Courses attracted working people in all the major industrial centers of England, among them London, Birmingham, Manchester, and Leeds.[45]

As the nineteenth century drew to a close, an emphatically non-egalitarian Friedrich Nietzsche infamously proclaimed and lamented what he found to be the unifying principle at work in the diversity of the modern mind: "God is dead."[46] Nietzsche understood perfectly well

---

[42]Ibid., 480-481 and 527-528.

[43]Everett Dean Martin, *The Meaning of a Liberal Education* (New York, NY: W. W. Norton, 1926), 256 and 254.

[44]Quoted in Curtis, *History of Education in Great Britain*, 408.

[45]Ibid., 455-459.

[46]"Could it be possible? This old saint in the forest has not heard anything of this, that *God is dead*?" Friedrich Nietzsche, *Thus Spoke Zarathustra*, in *The Portable Nietzsche*, trans. Walter Kaufmann (New York, NY: Penguin Books, 1982), 124.

that this alleged death encompassed the idea of humanity which was coeval with civilization itself; and with humanity, of course, must go the humanities or the liberal arts. *E Pluribus: Nihil*. This nihilism remains, consciously and unconsciously the dominant mode of thought in the teaching of what are still called the liberal arts in American universities. This fact is the source of the most challenging questions for teachers and students of the liberal arts today.

Conclusion

The tradition of the liberal arts is, in a decisive respect, the Western tradition, and the fate of the liberal arts will be inseparable from the fate of the West. The liberal arts came into formal and self-conscious being in the last glow of the political greatness of Athens and Greece. They were systematized as Rome reached and passed the apogee of its ancient pagan greatness. They were transformed by the centuries-long cultural and political spread of Christianity and again transformed by the rise to ascendancy of modern natural science. They are now patiently enduring deconstruction in the service of the dogmas of a passé postmodernism. There has always been—as there continues to be—lively disagreement about how the various disciplines are related to one another and, indeed, which are essential and why. This disagreement ascends to the greatest height of diversity: disagreement about the most urgent question—the question of the highest good, the question of the end or purpose of human existence. It is because of the seriousness of this question that the role of the liberal arts in Christian education in particular has been so hotly, often violently, disputed from the moment pagan philosophy and Christianity were first introduced to one another. We need not feel an undue sense of crisis if we find ourselves, on this small "bank and shoal of time," compelled again to ask basic if not simple questions. Is it not precisely our crisis that we have learned to ignore them?

Modern and Postmodern Challenges to Liberal Education

by Dennis A. Sheridan

Throughout the history of higher education, from medieval Europe to the present, many who have sought to advance Christian ideals through higher learning have done so through the vehicle of the liberal arts. Those disciplines which celebrate and refine human potential have been viewed by Christian scholars as powerful tools to advance the Kingdom of God. Today, although many American colleges and universities view their Christian identity as little more than historical legacy, some institutions have retained a commitment to provide higher education through the lens of a Christian worldview.[1]

DENNIS A. SHERIDAN is an associate professor of college student affairs and chair of the Department of College Student Affairs and Leadership Studies at Azusa Pacific University. He is a graduate of Louisiana Tech University (B.A.), Louisiana State University (M.Ed.), Southwestern Baptist Theological Seminary (M.R.E., Ed.D.), and University of California, Los Angeles (Ph.D.).

[1]There are presently more than 700 church-related institutions of higher education in the United States. They represent nearly one-fourth of all colleges and universities in the country and collectively enroll nearly ten percent of all students. Although these institutions vary in size from those with fewer than 500 students to those with more

These religious institutions share a common goal with their secular counterparts: developing well-educated, critical thinkers who can function effectively in a democracy. For the Christian institution, however, this social goal is ultimately subservient to the goal of preparing Christians for service to Christ and the world. These dual goals, as well as the historical contexts in which Christian colleges and universities have developed, have inspired a rich debate regarding the place of the liberal arts in contemporary Christian higher education. It is the purpose of this essay to outline the trends and developments of American higher education of the past century and a half which have had the greatest influence upon this debate. This will provide a context for the essays which follow as we think about the role of liberal education in preparing Christian leaders and servants in the twenty-first century.

A Brief Historical Introduction

Debate over curriculum in American higher education is not new. Since the founding of Harvard College in 1636, successive generations of academics have argued about who and what should be taught in America's diverse institutions of higher education. Until the mid-nineteenth century, the colleges which dotted America's landscape were unapologetically Christian, distinctively English, and decidedly classical.

The first serious deviations from this pattern were found in the University of Virginia, established in 1824 under the guidance of Thomas Jefferson, and in the University of the City of New York, opened in 1832 in the spirit of Jacksonian populism. Both institutions sought to create a new model of what American higher education should look like, Virginia by introducing the concept of electives within the curriculum, and New York by pursuing a utilitarian curriculum to serve the needs of a dynamic new nation. Both experiments incorporated aspects of an

---

than 20,000, the majority of church-related institutions are considered small colleges. Slightly more than half of these institutions would still be considered pervasively religious or religiously supportive. R. T. Sandin, *HEPS Profiles of Independent Higher Education*, 1:1 (Lake Forest, IL: Higher Education Planning Services, 1991). Cited in David S. Guthrie, "Mapping the Terrain of Church-Related Colleges and Universities," *New Directions for Higher Education*, no. 79 (San Francisco, CA: Jossey-Bass, 1992), 3-18.

emerging Germanic model of higher education with its emphasis on scientific inquiry.[2]

The threat posed by these and other early attempts at reform led the faculty of Yale College in 1828 to issue a stinging defense of the classical curriculum in American higher education. So strongly stated and widely accepted was the Yale Report of 1828 that serious attempts at reform in other institutions were delayed for a generation. The Yale Report provided a strong rationale for those whose primary interest was to keep America's colleges as they were—committed to the humanist, classical, and Christian traditions and resistant to the demands for a more popular and practical education.[3]

The emphasis on liberal education in American higher education of the early nineteenth century cannot be divorced from the equally important emphasis on piety. College presidents and faculty members alike were employed primarily for their religious faith and secondarily for their academic achievements. Prior to the Civil War, few American college professors could legitimately be called scholars. Many were clergymen or former clergymen, and the vast majority believed that "in serving the cause of knowledge and truth by promoting liberal education," they were serving the cause of the Christian faith.[4]

Following the Civil War, the American higher education landscape changed dramatically. By the dawn of the twentieth century, the pervasive changes in American society had taken their toll on the traditional American college. Scientific advances, urbanization, immigration, industrialization, increased wealth, the rising middle class, and increased mobility all contributed to a new consensus that new or re-made institutions were needed to give greater attention to the technical and practical and less attention to the religious and classical. The Morrill Federal Land Grant Act of 1862 (and the Second Morrill Act of 1890), perhaps more than any other effort, contributed to the creation of universities committed to practical courses of study for the growing American middle class.[5]

---

[2]Frederick Rudolph, *The American College and University: A History* (Athens, GA: University of Georgia Press, 1962, 1990), 124-130.

[3]Ibid., 134-135.

[4]Andrew Fleming West, *The Changing Conception of "The Faculty" in American Universities* (San Francisco, CA: 1906), 3. Cited in Rudolph, *The American College and University*, 159.

[5]Rudolph, *The American College and University*, 249.

According to Frederick Rudolph, the land-grant universities became in America "the temple of applied science, essentially institutionalizing the American's traditional respect for the immediately useful. . . . In the land-grant institutions the American people achieved popular higher education for the first time."[6]

Many other emerging institutions were as devoted to innovation as the land-grant colleges. Universities such as Cornell and Johns Hopkins contributed significantly to the shift in the ideal of what an American college or university should be. The emerging American university was devoted to the never-ending search for truth, using the scientific method as its primary tool. In contrast, the traditional American college "had all the truth it needed in revealed religion and in the humanist tradition."[7]

Among the educational leaders advocating reform in American higher education in the mid-nineteenth century, Francis Wayland of Brown University and Henry Tappan of the University of Michigan are exemplars. Both fulfilled prophetic roles in their advocacy for changes in higher education. Wayland argued that the classical curriculum was insufficient to the demands of the changing American society. According to George Marsden,

> Wayland saw that ultimately American university education would have to play a more vital social role and thus have a more tangible cash value on the bottom line. The outmoded colleges, which few Americans attended, were hardly going to lead the nation into a golden age of prosperity and moral and intellectual progress.[8]

In contrast to Wayland's practicality, Tappan was a romantic idealist who was among the first university presidents in America to have studied in Germany. His vision for American higher education was a scholarly and elite system which would identify and prepare wise leaders for the growing nation. As Tappan wrote, "This conception of education is not that of merely teaching men a trade, an art, or a profession; but that of

---

[6]Ibid., 265.

[7]Ibid., 274.

[8]George Marsden, *The Soul of the American University: From Protestant Establishment to Established Nonbelief* (New York, NY: Oxford University Press, 1994), 103.

quickening and informing souls with truths and knowledges [*sic*], and giving them the power of using all their faculties aright in whatever they choose to exert them."[9]

The Culture of Professionalism

Concurrent with these early shifts in American higher educational thought was a growing middle class with its emphasis on professionalism. Virtually no aspect of American life was exempt from this trend—popular culture, the academy, or even spectator sports. According to Burton Bledstein,

> Americans after 1870 . . . committed themselves to a culture of professionalism which over the years has established the thoughts, habits, and responses most modern Americans have taken for granted, a culture which has admirably served individuals who aspire to think very well of themselves.[10]

Middle-class life in America in the latter part of the nineteenth century became increasingly enamored with the idea of membership in a profession. The more respectable the demeanor, the greater the commitment to service, the more imposing the symbol of authority, the more theoretical the knowledge base, and the more elaborate the entrance ritual, the more *professional* the endeavor was considered to be. This growing professionalization of American society served a purpose in the order it provided and the sense of place it engendered. The resulting hierarchy of American life offered an emerging ideal of the American dream.

These changes in occupational status in American life placed new demands upon higher education institutions, both Christian and secular, to become more flexible and diverse. "Any occupation and any subculture

---

[9]Henry Tappan, *University Education* (New York, NY: G.P. Putnam, 1851), 13-14. Cited in Marsden, *The Soul of the American University*, 106.

[10]Burton J. Bledstein, *The Culture of Professionalism: The Middle Class and the Development of Higher Education in America* (New York, NY: W. W. Norton, 1978), 80-81.

of American life achieved recognition and status when it became deserving of study as a professional and academic science with its distinct theory and intellectual requirements."[11] The explosion of new areas of study in contemporary higher education (such as feminist studies, ethnic studies, leadership studies, criminal justice, and urban studies) are viewed by Bledstein as nothing more than an extension of a trend begun in the latter part of the nineteenth century. He observes, "When Mid-Victorians boldly defined such new subjects as sociology and American history, they only peeked at the possibilities of pluralism."[12]

American professionals of the late nineteenth century did not see the higher education debate as the elitist humanities versus the democratic natural sciences. According to Bledstein, they saw their struggle "in terms of professional studies versus practical ones, academic studies in any field versus on-the-job technical training, persons who discipline their minds versus persons who do not, qualified practitioners versus quacks."[13]

According to Bledstein, the structure of the culture of professionalism led to the structuring of American society in such a way that people could know and accept their rightful place in society. No one doubted that power, privilege, prestige, and money flowed upward in this vertical structure, ensuring that future generations of Americans would strive for upward mobility. In contrast to the European aristocracy, Americans used the objective measure of professional certification in order to identify and classify people. At least theoretically, no one in America needed to remain throughout their lives in the station to which they were born.[14]

German Influence on American Higher Education

During the latter part of the nineteenth century, the universities of Germany provided much of the graduate education pursued by American academicians. Between 1815 and 1914, nearly ten thousand Americans studied in Germany, and it would have been rare at the dawn of the

---

[11]Ibid., 125.

[12]Ibid.

[13]Ibid.

[14]Ibid.

twentieth century to find a major American scholar who had not studied in Germany.[15] Most scholars agree that the impact of this German influence was profound.

German higher education of the nineteenth century is usually noted for its emphasis on the scientific method, but the German approach to science was not quite the objective analytical approach typically assumed. German science, *Wissenschaft*, "was to take place within the context of philosophical idealism and could contribute to the larger humanistic goal of *Bildung*," the cultivation of character.[16] German academicians were quite content to pursue knowledge for its own sake and sought the cultivation of the objective *Geist*, the true inner self. Creative German scholars viewed knowledge and learning as a total effort in which the rational was not to remain isolated but connected in every conceivable fashion to the world. Their understanding of academic freedom was that the privileged academic class could pursue its abstract work unhindered by the government.[17]

While there was much about German higher education that should have been repulsive to Americans of the late nineteenth century—the elitism of the universities, the arrogance of the professoriate, the nationalism and anti-democratic attitudes of the academic culture—those who returned to the United States after studying there were zealous advocates of the power of the intellect to solve problems and make worldly applications of scientific technique. They saw in German scholarship an appreciation for the significance of ideas, the value of an active mind, and the willingness to be pioneers in specialized research.[18]

German-educated American scholars of the late nineteenth and early twentieth centuries sought then, in a uniquely American context, to establish scholarly activity as a true profession in its own right. In doing so, the *process* of scholarship came to be somewhat separated from the *content* of scholarship. Scholars could legitimately be found among those studying virtually *any* subject and not simply among those who pursued theology and the classics. President Tappan of the University of Michigan led the way in this transition. In working to recruit the brightest scholars

---

[15]Marsden, *The Soul of the American University*, 104.
[16]Ibid., 105.
[17]Bledstein, *The Culture of Professionalism*, 316-317.
[18]Ibid.

for his institution, Tappan identified "professionalism" as the essential quality in faculty hiring.[19] All of higher education followed suit, including Christian colleges and universities.

Another effect of the German model was the diversification of the curricula of America's colleges and universities. As the twentieth century approached, increasing diversification in subject-matter and fields of study was evident as doctorally trained faculty members concentrated on their narrowly drawn areas of scholarship. Where the old-time college professor had been a generalist, the modern college professor was a specialist. Faculties were increasingly divided and sub-divided into departments and schools. The bureaucracy of the university became increasingly complex.[20]

Education for What? The Value of Utility

America during the late nineteenth century was a nation fast becoming a great industrial power. "To ensure access to the expanding opportunities for wealth and economic security in this kind of highly competitive society, young people . . . were coming to demand that the colleges offer . . . 'practical' pre-vocational professional courses so that they might be prepared to take advantage of these opportunities."[21] Liberal arts colleges followed the lead of the public universities in responding to these demands. The financial incentives, both from increased tuition and from major donors, proved too strong for most institutions to resist the trend.

A study of the curricula in America's colleges between 1825 and 1905 revealed dramatic changes over the course of the nineteenth century. Among these changes were (1) the introduction of numerous new fields of study, such as modern languages and the sciences; (2) the introduction of an elective system, both in terms of majors and minors and in the selection of individual courses; (3) an abandonment of required study in ancient languages; (4) the introduction of courses previously considered vocational; and (5) the emergence of the Bachelor of Science degree.[22]

---

[19]Ibid., 107.

[20]Willis Rudy, *The Evolving Liberal Arts Curriculum: A Historical Review of Basic Themes* (New York, NY: Teachers College, Columbia University, 1960), 8-9.

[21]Ibid., 7.

[22]Ibid., 9.

According to Willis Rudy, the radical changes in the college curriculum during the late nineteenth century was a natural reflection of the drastic changes taking place in American society, in particular, the transformation from a rural to an industrial economy. "The new times necessitated new ways of living and thinking. The watchwords of the era were now progress, competition, and material expansion. Thus, the revolution in the curriculum was produced by a revolution in American life."[23]

The trend towards an increasingly pragmatic curriculum gained momentum near the end of the nineteenth century and became even more magnified in the years during and immediately following the First World War. Industrialization, urbanization, the rise of the sciences, the influence of German universities, and the increasing demand for specialized skills were responsible for dramatic changes in the college curriculum. Students flocked to colleges and universities in record numbers, so that by the middle of the twentieth century, roughly one-fourth of the college-aged population was in attendance. This compared to less than one-half of one percent attending a century before. Higher education in the early twentieth century came to be viewed by many as a necessity for upward mobility rather than as a luxury available to the upper classes. The new college students of the twentieth century demanded curricula which were specifically career-related in a professionally oriented society.[24]

By 1925, the curriculum of the typical American college or university would have been nearly unrecognizable to the authors of the Yale Report of 1828. While not totally abandoning the liberal arts, most colleges and universities had increasingly focused their attention on specialized courses of study designed to prepare students for careers. The advent of experimental psychology contributed to changed views of the role of learners in the learning process so that the rigors of the classical curriculum were not necessarily viewed as the only means by which the mind could be developed. These developments contributed to a notion that professionally oriented programs might be equally as useful as classical studies in achieving the aims of traditional liberal education.[25]

---

[23]Ibid., 11.
[24]Ibid., 36.
[25]Ibid., 38.

Pragmatism: A New Philosophy for the Twentieth Century

The philosophy of pragmatism has dominated American education for most of the twentieth century. Any discussion of the role of liberal education in American society is incomplete without an examination of the development of this critical philosophical system and its impact on American educational practice.

For the pragmatist, education is viewed as the chief means by which society strengthens, perfects, and perpetuates itself. As such, education then relies on society to determine for itself what the ultimate aims of educational endeavors are to be. In pragmatism, *society* is the ultimate authority for determining what is true, what is real, and what is of value (the three basic questions of philosophy). Rather than seeking to reflect ultimate ideals as the sources of truth and reality (as would the idealist), the pragmatist seeks to reflect the ideals of society. Thus, education becomes the primary means for the pursuit of social ideals.[26]

Pragmatists strongly advocate that the purpose of the educational system is to bring about change and the restructuring of society. They view educational institutions as agents of change which exist to challenge learners to develop solutions to complex societal problems. Traditionalists believe just as strongly that the purpose of education is to preserve the cultural heritage of society and transmit this heritage to subsequent generations. In this view, the determination of *what* should be taught and learned through formal education should take place *outside* the educational arena and imported only after very careful and deliberate debate.

For the pragmatist, the standard by which educational content and practice should be judged is the ethic of democracy, the cornerstones of which are commitment to the sanctity of the individual, tolerance for differences in belief and opinion, majority rule with minority rights, and provisions for changing the system through peaceful means. Pragmatists hold that American educational institutions are responsible for developing commitments and attitudes which support these ideals.

---

[26]I am indebted to Gordon Lee for this discussion of pragmatic philosophy. See Gordon C. Lee, *Education and Democratic Ideals: Philosophical Backgrounds of Modern Educational Thought* (New York, NY: Harcourt, Brace, 1965), 109-121.

For the traditionalist, the standard by which educational content and practice should be judged is its commitment to those dimensions of civilization which have survived the test of time. The basic authority for educational programs in the Western world have been the Christian and the classical traditions, embodied in the scholastic and humanistic approaches to education. While the pragmatist is primarily concerned with today's world and the immediate situation, the traditionalist stresses the permanent and the transcendent.

Pragmatism and Higher Education in the Late Twentieth Century

American higher education has been pulled in the direction of pragmatism throughout the twentieth century. This trend came into full flower in the years following World War II as dramatic changes took place in America's colleges and universities. The extent to which higher education has been well-served by pragmatic philosophy is easily seen in the dramatic enrollment increases, enhanced access for those previously excluded from higher education, greater involvement with both government and business, the incorporation of free-market strategies into the business of higher education, and increased specialization in curricular offerings—developments affecting most Christian and secular campuses.

The theme of access is quite congruent with the philosophy of pragmatism, for its adherents hold that society benefits from broad access to higher education. In 1947, there were approximately 2.3 million college students studying in more than 1,800 postsecondary institutions in the United States. Of this number, roughly half were in public institutions and half were in private institutions.[27] By 1991, this number had increased to roughly 14.2 million students in 4,500 institutions, only 22% of whom were enrolled in private institutions. By 2003, it is estimated that there

[27]Raymond Walters, "Statistics of Attendance in American Universities and Colleges, 1949," *School and Society* 70 (December 1949), 392. Cited in Christopher J. Lucas, *American Higher Education: A History* (New York, NY: St. Martin's Press, 1994), 227-231.

will be between 15 and 16 million students studying in America's postsecondary institutions.[28]

Within these growing numbers can be found larger percentages of female students, students from minority ethnic groups, older students, and graduate students. Between 1976 and 1988, college enrollments increased 13% for Caucasian students, 9% for African American students, 77% for Latino students, 151% for Asian American students, and 22% for Native American students.[29] Between 1970 and 1991, the number of women in college more than doubled, and in 1989, women received 53% of all baccalaureate degrees granted in the United States. The number of graduate students increased nearly 30% between 1978 and 1991. In 1991, about 45% of all college students were over the age of twenty-four.[30]

Following World War II, the federal government became increasingly involved as a major player in American higher education. With this enhanced role came increased funding and increased control. The Servicemen's Readjustment Act of 1944 (commonly referred to as the G. I. Bill) and Public Law 550 of 1952 (which provided billions of dollars for returning war veterans to pursue higher education) were only the beginning of what ultimately became a flood of federal dollars into America's colleges and universities. The Higher Education Facilities Act of 1963, the National Defense Education Act of 1958, and the Higher Education Acts of 1965 and 1972 (as well as their subsequent reauthorizations) are examples of the broad involvement of the federal government into higher education by providing money for classrooms, laboratories, libraries, student aid, and research.[31] As the country's institutions of higher education became increasingly dependent on federal funding, they also became obligated to comply with a growing list of regulations which accompanied the flow of dollars. As with greater access,

---

[28]Thomas D. Snyder, et al., *Digest of Educational Statistics 1993* (Washington, D.C.: National Center for Educational Statistics, October 1993), 172-223. Cited in Lucas, *American Higher Education: A History*, 227-231.

[29]B. Astone and E. Nunez-Wormack, "Population Trends, Socioeconomic Status, and Geographic Distribution," in F. K. Stage et al., *College Students: The Evolving Nature of Research* (Needham Heights, MA: Simon and Schuster Custom Publishing, 1996), 4-17.

[30]Snyder, et al., *Digest of Educational Statistics 1993*, 172-223. Cited in Lucas, *American Higher Education: A History*, 227-231.

[31]Ibid.

the increased involvement of the federal government in higher education poses no great contradiction for the pragmatist. Any compromises which have to be made in terms of institutional mission or purpose are well worth the price in order to achieve other goals.

In a similar vein, America's colleges and universities have become deeply involved with corporate America in recent decades. Most often this involvement has been in the form of funded research designed to produce marketable results. As corporations have shared their profits with the universities they fund, alliances have emerged which have raised questions about the "purity" of the mission of higher education. According to historian Page Smith, "Let us pray that we . . . will hear no more pious pronouncements about the universities' being engaged in the 'pursuit of truth.' What they are clearly pursuing with far more dedication than the truth is big bucks."[32] In 1996 alone, more than $330 million were earned in royalties on licenses granted by the nation's top one hundred research universities. Among all colleges, there were nearly five thousand licenses which were income producing.[33] Clearly, American higher education has become deeply involved in the development of products for the marketplace, a state of affairs entirely consistent with the philosophy of pragmatism.

American higher education has accepted far more than funding from corporate America; it has also adopted its model of government. During the past thirty or forty years, colleges and universities have become increasingly complex bureaucracies. They have struggled to balance the demands of quality with the demands for efficiency while having had placed upon them greater and greater demands for accountability. They appear to have wholeheartedly embraced the corporate ethic of the free market to the point that many institutions have taken on all of the characteristics of a large corporation.[34]

As the corporate model has changed the face of higher education, competition has become increasingly pervasive. Students must compete for admission, for seats in classes, for grades, for financial aid, and,

---

[32]Page Smith, *Killing the Spirit: Higher Education in America* (New York, NY: Viking Penguin, 1990), 13.

[33]Goldie Blumenstyk, "Royalties on Inventions Bring $336-Million to Top U.S. Research Universities," *The Chronicle of Higher Education,* 27 February 1998, A44.

[34]Lucas, *American Higher Education: A History*, 237-240.

ultimately, for jobs. Faculty members likewise compete for employment, for tenure, for promotion, for salary enhancements, for research grants, for sabbaticals, for office and work space, and for recognition. Departments or divisions within an institution compete for space, funding, and administrative support. And institutions themselves compete vigorously with one another for students and the tuition dollars they provide. Those institutions with a reputation for success are most likely to be those which have been successful in building an image, responding to market demands for educational programs, and positioning themselves carefully in relation to their competitors.[35] With such competition abounding, there is little wonder that the ultimate purposes for which most institutions were founded have become lost or muted. Pragmatism is thriving in American higher education.

But it is in the curriculum where the ultimate tension between pragmatic and traditional voices has been felt most intensely. While the pragmatists have urged specialization, diversification, and inclusion, the traditionalists have argued for commonality, coherence, and preservation. We see, on the one hand, efforts to provide unity and coherence in higher education through a core curriculum that is shared by everyone and, on the other, the recognized need to continually restructure the curriculum to introduce new perspectives, new specialties, and new responses to the needs of a changing society.[36]

The nature of the debate is easily seen in the conflicting positions during the late 1930s between traditionalists such as Robert Maynard Hutchins and Mortimer Adler and pragmatists such as John Dewey and William James. The traditionalists argued that modern society, with its ethical relativism and secularism, would find true education in the wisdom of the past. They loudly proclaimed that American higher education was being driven away from its search for truth in its pursuit of scientific, practical, and vocational ends. The pragmatists, led by John Dewey, emphasized that education is best constructed by providing students with experiences in seeking solutions to present social and personal problems. Dewey criticized the traditionalists for their beliefs in fixed truth and fixed human nature.[37]

---

[35]Ibid.

[36]Ibid.

[37]Marsden, *The Soul of the American University*, 379-380.

In 1945, a faculty committee at Harvard University published a report called *General Education in a Free Society*, commonly referred to as the "Redbook," because of the color of its binding.[38] The Harvard Redbook, while ultimately rejected by the faculty of Harvard, was widely acclaimed as a balanced and articulate expression on the meaning of general education, which they equated with liberal education. The report called for a balance of both general and specialized education, claiming that both were essential in a free society. The aim of higher education in modern society, urged the report, was "the development of the educated person—an individual capable of thinking effectively, communicating clearly, making relevant judgments, and discriminating with care among values."[39] While insisting that general education should not be thought of as a set course of study or collection of books, the ancient ideal of liberal education should be extended as far as possible to all members of society.[40] In this sense, the Harvard Redbook essentially supported the position taken by other traditionalists.

A slightly different approach was taken by Horace M. Kallen in *The Education of Free Men* in 1949. Kallen insisted that any form of learning qualifies as liberal education if it aids in liberating a student's mind from the provincialism of his or her place and time. From his perspective, the aim of liberal education is "to teach people to learn about one another, to understand, respect, and appreciate differences among themselves, and to assist them in working together for common ends."[41]

The Great Depression, World War II, the space race of the 1950s and 1960s (spurred by successful launching of the Sputnik satellite), and the Cold War all served to reinforce the place of pragmatism in American higher education. Technical proficiency and expertise were viewed as the means by which America could sustain its place in the international community and stem the tide of Soviet expansion. For many, general education became a luxury and not a necessity. Specialization and

---

[38]See *General Education in a Free Society* (Cambridge, MA: Harvard University Press, 1945).

[39]Cited in Lucas, *American Higher Education: A History*, 251.

[40]Ibid.

[41]Horace M. Kallen, *The Education of Free Men* (New York, NY: Farrar, Straus, and Giroux, 1949), 325-326. Cited in Lucas, *American Higher Education: A History*, 252.

professionalism were needed to preserve the country's position of world leadership.[42]

From Pragmatism to Postmodernism

Following the turmoil of the 1960s and 1970s, America's college campuses returned to a state of relative tranquillity. This provided an opportunity to take a new look at the role of higher education in society, including the place of liberal education. Many competing voices joined in the debate. Some urged a more global and international perspective; others argued that morality and ethics needed greater attention; still others encouraged curricular solutions to the growing problem of narcissism in the younger generation. From whatever perspective they came, however, there was considerable consensus that there was a significant problem eating away at the soul of American higher education. In 1971, a Commission on Liberal Learning of the American Association of American Colleges issued a report which asserts,

> Contemporary liberal education seems irrelevant to much of the undergraduate population and, more especially, to middle America. The concept of intellect has not been democratized; the humanities are moribund, unrelated to student interest, and the liberal arts appear headed for stagnation. Narrow vocational education has captured the larger portion of political interest. . . . The liberal arts are captives of illiberally educated faculty members who barter with credit hours and pacts of nonaggression among their fiefs and baronies. Illiberally educated politicians, who want a bigger gross national product with scant regard for whether the minds and lives of the persons who produce it are or are not gross, make their own negative contribution, as do illiberally educated students.[43]

In the disorientation and confusion of this era, there emerged a philosophical system which in subsequent years came to be known as postmodernism, defined and understood by many as a contrast with the

---

[42]Lucas, *American Higher Education: A History*, 253-255.

[43]Willis D. Weatherford, "Commission on Liberal Learning," *Liberal Education* 57, no. 2 (1971): 37.

"modern" (i.e., pragmatic) philosophy it seeks to replace. The ultimate impact of postmodernism on liberal education may not be fully known for quite some time. In fact, Harland Bloland laments that the scholarship on higher education has grossly neglected the subject.[44] However, postmodernism is in fact at the center of contemporary higher education debates on the nature of truth, reality, and the structure of society (including the role of education).

While the meaning of the terms "modern" and "postmodern" are inconsistently understood, it is still possible to draw broad comparisons between the two. Both modernism and postmodernism strive to make meaning of the cultural, economic, political, and social changes taking place in art, architecture, literature, the social sciences, popular culture, industry, business, technology, and education. Modernism is committed to logic, reason, and the scientific method and assumes that these are the tools that lead to truth and reality. Modernists have long believed that the scientific method is capable of producing solutions to the problems of the world and that there are no limits to where the search for truth may lead. They equate change with progress and believe that democracy leads to freedom, equality, justice, and prosperity. For modernists, education and professionalism are seen as keys to upward mobility and the attainment of the American dream.[45] To the extent that today's universities are deeply rooted in modernist views and values, they pursue two major goals: (1) producing autonomous, critically reasoning individuals; and (2) producing knowledge that has immediate and powerful application in the world.[46]

But there is a darker side to modernism which is the object of much of the criticism aimed its way by the postmodernists. Modernism has produced rampant materialism, a consumer society, a ravaged environment, and unrestrained technology. It can be associated with oppression, exploitation, repression, violence, and even terror. For the postmodernist, higher education is culpable as an accessory to these crimes.

---

[44]See Harland G. Bloland, "Postmodernism and Higher Education," *Journal of Higher Education* 66, no. 5 (1995): 521-560.

[45]Ibid.

[46]John E. Willis, Jr. "The Post-Postmodern University," *Change* 27, no. 2 (1995), 59-63.

Postmodernism is closely associated with poststructuralism which developed in France in the 1970s. It focuses upon the "indeterminacy of language, the primacy of discourse, the decentering and fragmentation of the concept of self, the significance of the 'other,' a recognition of the . . . unbreakable power/knowledge nexus, the attenuation of a belief in metanarratives, and the decline of dependence upon rationalism."[47]

Much of postmodernism's orientation centers on language and how it is used. Jacques Derrida is a seminal postmodernist who introduced the role of deconstruction in challenging the assumptions of modernism. For Derrida, the meanings of words are constantly changing from one social setting to another and from one person to another. The strategy of deconstruction involves close examination of texts to reveal concealed hierarchies, hidden oppositions, inconsistencies, and contradictions. In deconstruction, the central arguments of a text are ignored in the search for what has been neglected, omitted, or withheld.[48]

As applied to higher education, deconstruction seeks to identify and expose all of the hidden hierarchies (whether real or perceived) present within the system. This could involve the assumed superiority of the "hard" sciences over the "soft" sciences, of the liberal arts over professional programs, of graduate programs over undergraduate programs, and of research over teaching. This could involve the assumption that students are subservient to professors who are in turn subservient to administrators.[49] Each of these hierarchies, postmodernists argue, is nothing more than a social construction which marginalizes and excludes people and their ideas. They further argue that the history of Western civilization is characterized by tendencies to silence differences and exclude outsiders. The result has been an academic canon dominated by white males which has excluded the perspectives and experiences of women, ethnic minorities, homosexuals, and non-theists.

As higher education is further deconstructed by postmodernists, the scientific method comes under special scrutiny and criticism. They see science and its emphasis on creativity, objectivity, and neutrality as ultimately responsible for the hierarchies and the reward structure of the

---

[47]Bloland, "Postmodernism and Higher Education," 524.
[48]Ibid.
[49]Ibid.

academy. Even the humanities are driven by scientific notions of discovery, objectivity, and cumulative knowledge. Postmodernists abhor the misguided notion that the search for truth is largely defined in scientific terms. They view science as a discourse (a metanarrative) like any other in which power struggles take place for the control of meaning. It is not the objective, value-free form of knowledge it pretends to be but is greatly affected by social and political values. In this sense, postmodernists view science as no more or less important than creationism or astrology.[50] From their perspective, every discourse, regardless of its merit, has a place in the curricula of colleges and universities. According to this view, there are no standards by which the academy may judge the relative merits of curricular offerings. Questions of inclusion or exclusion are reduced to power struggles of contesting points of view. In the postmodern world, everything is political, everything is relative.

Particularly significant to the discussion of the effect of postmodernism on liberal education is the notion of implosion, espoused by the French postmodernist Jean Baudrillard. In implosion, the boundaries which separate reality and simulation disappear, eliminating any basis for judging what is real. Bloland illustrates this concept by offering comparisons of politicians with the images of them created by the media. The difficulty in distinguishing between that which is real and that which is image represents the implosion of the boundary separating the two.[51]

For higher education in general and liberal education in particular, this kind of implosion has serious consequences for the organization, the purposes, and the activities of the university. In the truly postmodern university, there would be no boundaries between knowledge inside the academy and outside it (thus ending the university's monopoly on knowledge); there would be no limit on what should be included in the curriculum (for there are no criteria for determining what is valuable and what is not); and even the distinctions between academic disciplines would eventually become meaningless and disappear.[52]

---

[50]Ibid.
[51]Ibid.
[52]Ibid.

Rethinking Liberal Education in a Postmodern World

There is much about postmodernism which poses a serious threat to traditional liberal arts education. The first and most important of these threats is the exclusion of the possibility of absolute truth. The postmodernist views all notions of absolute goodness, truth, and justice as anachronistic, particularly if these are understood as deriving from an eternal and unchanging God. Second, postmodernists view reality as a relative concept. All individuals have their own reality because they experience the world through their unique cultural, political, religious, social, and personal lenses. For the postmodernist, perception is indeed reality, and no one has the right to impose upon anyone else a standard of what is real, what is true, what is good, what is just, and what is valuable. Finally, postmodernism offers a pessimistic view of life which is devoid of hope. It views human beings as limited and lonely and human existence as random and transitory. Nothing or no one is to be trusted; nothing should shock or disturb; coherence and meaning are illusive.[53]

While there is much in postmodernism that is antithetical to traditional liberal arts education in general and Christian liberal arts education in particular, there are perhaps several insights which might be instructive as we strive to redefine the role of liberal education in contemporary Christian higher education. First, postmodernism seeks to retain some of the mystery of human existence which modern science has sought to eliminate. It can perhaps help rescue for academia the possibility of human beings having religious or spiritual needs that cannot be satisfied through the objective, scientific approach to life. Since Christian educators have never abandoned their belief in the spiritual dimension, this could provide an avenue of congruence between Christian higher education and the secular academy.

Second, postmodernism actually serves to open the academy to the voices of Christian scholars and others with a theistic approach to teaching and scholarship. If all views are considered equal in a postmodern world, then the Christian voice must be as welcomed as any other.

Third, postmodernism can help rescue the voices of those who have indeed been oppressed, excluded, or marginalized. The academy should

---

[53]Joseph J. Feeney, "Can a Worldview Be Healed? Students and Postmodernism," *America,* 15 November 1997, 12-16.

not be closed to learning from those whose experiences have not been in the mainstream of Western thought. Christian educators in particular should be advocates of inclusion in light of the message of the Christian gospel and should not be afraid to offer scholarly critique of the abuses of power and establishmentarianism.

Finally, postmodernism can teach us that objectifying truth and holding it at arm's length is dangerous and inhuman. The search for truth is never value-neutral and totally objective. Recognizing, identifying, and even celebrating the values, assumptions, and perspectives we bring to teaching and scholarship can enrich and expand the meaningfulness of our work.

Those involved in Christian higher education have a wonderful opportunity to become engaged in serious conversations regarding issues of who should be taught, what they should be taught, how they should be taught, and by whom they should be taught. Many students come to Christian institutions with postmodern assumptions and values, and many Christian institutions have adopted (perhaps unknowingly) elements of postmodernist thinking. This creates an opportunity, as well as a responsibility, to re-examine and re-affirm those enduring values which make Christian higher education unique. Joseph Feeney offers an eloquent reminder that Christian institutions have a unique opportunity to adopt a healing role in American undergraduate education:

> As an intellectual experience, [Christian higher education] can examine different worldviews and clarify their underlying values and presuppositions. As a humanistic education, it can probe what it means to be human and offer a coherent worldview that includes both meaning and the spiritual. As Christian education, it offers a living God, redemption in Christ, a community of believers, and hope for this world and in eternity. . . . [Furthermore] it can help students discover God through all creation, seek intellectual integration, work for the greater good and stand with people most in need. . . . [It] can restore students' ability to feel by enabling them to serve the needy and so feel how much they are needed. Thus, we might hope, comes healing and hope for both worldviews and students.[54]

---

[54]Ibid., 16.

Integrating Liberal Arts and Professional Education

by Phillip V. Lewis and Rosemary Liegler

A liberal arts education strives to reflect the breadth of human culture, enlighten human thought, and promote deeper understanding of the world in which we live.[1] Such an education, oriented toward the development of the whole person, has been called the foundation of American democracy. Steven Sample describes liberal learning as the

---

PHILLIP V. LEWIS is professor of management and dean of the School of Business and Management at Azusa Pacific University. He is a graduate of Abilene Christian College (B.S.), University of Denver (M.A.), and University of Houston (Ed.D.). **ROSEMARY LIEGLER** is professor of nursing and dean of the School of Nursing at Azusa Pacific University. She is a graduate of St. Ambrose College (BSN), Marquette University (MSN), and Claremont Graduate School (Ph.D.).

[1]A variety of definitions for "liberal arts" exists. We accept the definition proposed by the editors of this volume. However, in this article, no distinctions are made among "liberal arts education," "liberal learning," "liberal studies," or "liberal education." Liberal learning is sometimes said to be the sum of general education, specialized education, and the co-curriculum; however, as David Baird suggests, the reality is far more complex: "Liberal learning is not a mathematical formula that can be calculated according to units, hours, and courses. As a process, the whole is always greater than its parts." "Opportunities for Liberal Learning in the Twenty-First Century" (Malibu, CA: Pepperdine University, 1997), 15.

intellectual core of a university education.[2] John Buchan suggests that a liberal education should endow a recipient with humility, humanity, and humor.[3] Lee Gruget says that "liberal education calls higher education always to its mission of enriching the human mind and spirit. The learner is liberated from narrow thinking to recognize connections among many ideas. And always the ethical is injected into consideration of the immediately practical."[4]

These scholars assume a positive, rich, and complex perspective on the liberal arts. On the other hand, there is a common tendency to approach them in terms of a shallow dichotomy. *Encyclopaedia Britannica*, for example, defines liberal arts education as "a curriculum aimed at imparting general knowledge and developing general intellectual capacities *in contrast to* a professional, vocational or technical curriculum (emphasis added)."[5] There has been a traditional conviction that liberal arts education must shun professional studies because of the latter's apparent narrowness and inherently practical nature. Such has been the debate for decades, creating tensions on many college campuses and resulting in a bimodal culture.

Critics of professional education, however, often ignore changes that have taken place in recent decades. In the 1960s, for example, widespread change in professional school curriculums occurred after funded reports made recommendations about needed revisions designed to strengthen programs of study.[6] Complaints about professional schools before these studies suggested they were vocational, mostly descriptive, overly focused on business-past, and insufficiently based on mathematics and science. Although the studies made useful recommendations that included the

---

[2]Steven B. Sample, "The Great Straddlers—Successors to the Renaissance Man," *Liberal Education* 81, no. 4 (1995): 54-57.

[3]John Buchan, *Harvard Alumni Bulletin* (July 1938), 143, as quoted in Henry Rosovsky, *The University: An Owner's Manual* (New York, NY: W. W. Norton, 1990), 101.

[4]Lee E.Grugel, "Our Phrase of Choice," *Liberal Education* 81, no. 2 (1995): 50-52.

[5]*Encyclopaedia Britannica*, 15th ed., 6:195. Quoted in Rosovsky, *The University,* 99-100.

[6]In business, those studies included the Gordon-Howell report, funded by the Ford Foundation, and the Pierson report, funded by the Carnegie Corporation of New York; both reports were released in 1959. These studies were updated by Porter and McKibbin in 1988, having been so commissioned by the American Assembly of Collegiate Schools of Business.

requirement of a strong liberal arts background for undergraduates, the resulting restructuring of professional programs has had little effect on the negative attitudes of liberal arts faculty toward professional schools.

This state of being at odds with one another is a consequence of the contrasting goals of each type of education. However, such tension is unnecessary. What is needed instead is mutual understanding that results in the thoughtful integration of these seemingly divergent fields. As it stands, *liberal arts* is said to comprise knowledge for the sake of knowledge. It is an education that prepares students to live. Its quality of life deals with ideas, not monetary gain. On the other hand, *professional studies* is said to involve knowledge for the sake of occupation. It is a vocational education that prepares students to make a living. Its quality of life deals with monetary gain, not ideas. We would argue that neither of these overly simplified approaches contributes insight to either field, and that such narrow perspectives do little to relieve any of the tension.

Perceived conflicts and tensions have been exacerbated by recent cultural shifts. For the fall of 1967 class of incoming freshman, 82.5% considered "development of a meaningful philosophy" as highly important. Fewer than 41% thought "being very well off financially" was important. Thirty years later, the 1997 class completely reversed those percentages.[7] Peter Schrag says the likely explanation for the economic orientation of this generation "is that the educational system has failed in not enabling these presumptive citizens to place themselves in the context of the larger society."[8] Alexander Astin, who heads the UCLA Higher Education Research Institute, concludes, "This is a generation not of apathetic ingrates, but of people who are simply undereducated."[9]

The UCLA study presents a challenge to both liberal and professional educators. We suggest it raises the following questions:

1. When parents send their children to a university to receive an education, do they also assume their children will be able to get a job upon graduation?

---

[7]According to a survey by the Higher Education Research Institute at UCLA summarized in Peter Schrag, "Why Aren't Students Interested in Learning?" *The Los Angeles Times,* 8 February 1998, sec. A, p. 17.

[8]Ibid.

[9]Ibid.

2. If a student is unable to make a living upon graduation, what value was offered to either the student or the parents?
3. If a student is able get a job but knows little about life, what value was added to his/her education?
4. Are we offering majors which have potential for being an occupational hazard to a student's future?

It should be noted that most businesses oppose the mass-production mentality and favor a worker-collaborative approach. Therefore, they are likely to hire on the basis of a person's ability to integrate professional specialization and practicality with the ability to live life appropriately, rendering the above questions outdated and shortsighted.

Today's professional studies programs encourage people to act responsibly and live lives of quality. Their focused expertise is likewise aimed toward service to society. Liberal education has not cornered the market on such virtues, as Madeleine Grumet emphasizes in her description of quality professional education: "Bearing the burden and dignity for intervening in other people's lives, their learning, health, and worldly affairs, professionals are educated to develop the ethics and discipline their practice requires."[10] Given this more accurate, more well-rounded understanding, it would seem that the purposes of these two educational cultures are quite compatible. To further emphasize this point, Peter Drucker offers the following illustration:

> To be sure, management, like any other work, has its own tools and its own techniques. But just as the essence of medicine is not the urinalysis, important though it is, the essence of management is not techniques and procedures. The essence of management is to make knowledge productive. Management, in other words, is a social function. And in its practice, management is truly a "liberal art."[11]

A professional education is incomplete if it does not prepare its graduates to live satisfying lives and pursue their work with integrity,

---

[10]Madeleine R. Grumet, "Education with Purpose," *Liberal Education* 81, no. 1 (1995), 4-11.

[11]Peter F. Drucker, *Managing in a Time of Great Change* (San Francisco, CA: Jossey-Bass, 1995), 250.

responsibility, and compassion. Similarly, a liberal arts education is incomplete if it does not prepare educated people to thrive in the professional world. Both disciplines "can and should look to each other for new frameworks, strategies of inquiry, and modes of learning."[12]

The Rise of and Demand for Professional Education

To accurately pinpoint the beginnings of professional education is somewhat difficult. Drucker, for example, traces management as a *practice* back some 4,700 years to that Egyptian who first conceived the pyramid.[13] However, as a *discipline*, management emerged in the United States during World War II to become the fastest-growing new discipline in the last sixty years.[14] The demand for and salaries paid to graduates of these programs also rose rapidly, which did little to help build relationships between the professional schools and underpaid liberal arts faculty.

Other writers suggest that the need for professional schools began some time around 1900 as we began to lose the possibility of comprehensive and fully integrated knowledge of our world. The invention of movable type, the Industrial Revolution, and an expanded emphasis on a visual environment resulted in an incredible increase in the rate of change. Knowledge has exploded—someone's facetious comment that Goethe was the last man who knew everything may in fact be true.[15] The world today is as different from the world in which we were born as that world was from Julius Caesar's. Almost as much has happened since we were born as had happened before. This shock of discontinuity, coupled with the ability to process, manipulate, and store data at incredible rates, gave impetus to the need for and emergence of new specializations.

---

[12]Joseph Johnston, *Beyond Borders: Profiles in International Education* (Washington D.C.: American Association of Colleges and American Assembly of Collegiate Schools of Business, 1993).

[13]Drucker, *Managing in a Time of Great Change*, 25.

[14]In less than ten years overlapping the 1960s and 1970s, fifty new Ph.D. programs were established in business administration. Unfortunately, many of the graduates from these programs had no idea how to attack real-world business problems and could communicate only with their colleagues.

[15]Sample, "The Great Straddlers—Successors to the Renaissance Man," 54-57.

Thus, in recent times the professions have achieved a peculiar hegemony in the intellectual life of universities. The professional school model has integrated itself into the arts and sciences because it represents a way of doing meaningful intellectual work in a period of almost incomprehensible expansion and the increasing fragmentation of knowledge.[16] The intellectual energy released within both fields, as professors seek to bridge the gap between disparate ideas and modes of thinking, can result in dramatic discoveries and encounters.

A Two-Culture Phenomenon: Liberal v. Professional Education

Promoting the integration of liberal studies and professional education is of utmost importance as we prepare competent future practitioners. The demands upon practitioners in the twenty-first century require new approaches to solve complex problems, and a heightened capacity for critical thinking and informed reasoning in a constantly changing environment.[17] Faculty teaching in the professional fields, as well as professional organizations and commissions, reinforce the importance of this integration by identifying the critical competencies and outcomes professional education has in common with liberal education.[18] While a liberal education gives value to a professional vocation and offers meaning to the world of work, professional studies also offer relevant experiences to students in liberal education courses.[19]

---

[16]Ibid.

[17]Ernest A. Lynton, "New Concepts of Professional Expertise: Liberal Learning as Part of Career-Oriented Education," working paper no. 4, (Boston, MA: New England Resource Center for Higher Education, 1990). James L. McDowell, "Increasing the Liberal Arts Content of Professional/Technical Curriculum," (paper presented at the Annual Conference of the Association for General and Liberal Studies, Daytona Beach, Fla., October 1996).

[18]Joan S. Stark, "Liberal Education and Professional Programs: Conflict, Coexistence, or Compatibility?" In *Creating Career Programs in a Liberal Arts Context*, New Directions for Higher Education, no. 57, ed. Mary Ann F. Rehnke (1987): 91-102. Joan S. Stark and Malcolm A. Lowther, *Strengthening the Ties That Bind: Integrating Undergraduate Liberal and Professional Study,* report of the Professional Preparation Network (Ann Arbor, MI: Professional Preparation Network, 1988).

[19]Ernest L. Boyer, *College: The Undergraduate Experience in America* (New York, NY: Harper and Row, 1987).

Michael Useem suggests that liberal learning is a high-octane platform for entering the professions, with changes in education and careers that reshape one another.[20] In a knowledge-intensive environment, where business is global, competition challenging, and change unrelenting, a liberal arts foundation helps prepare working professionals for a rapidly changing organizational environment. The change from the Industrial Age to the Information Age, from product to knowledge, calls for different organizations and workers. It also suggests that the only way to manage change may be by intentional risk-taking.

The nature of the professions in the twenty-first century necessitates a changing practitioner in our ever-changing environment.[21] In reality, professional practice frequently differs from carrying out the controlled experiments emphasized in our educational programs. As Lynton says,

> In business, government, health care, social sciences, education and most other spheres of professional activity, reality is messy, problems are not well defined, and instead of unique solutions there exists in most situations a variety of options, each involving trade-offs among competing goals and values.[22]

Many different factors affect a given situation in professional practice—the ethical and moral component, environmental and economic considerations, as well as the cultural norms of the profession and the individuals involved. Professionals in health care fields frequently encounter these competing goals and values. For example, research has determined clear guidelines for removing a mechanical ventilator that is needed for respiratory assistance. When a defined level of plasma oxygen concentration is achieved and when a patient can breathe without assistance, he or she can be removed from the ventilator. In real life situations, however, patients fear breathing without mechanical assistance and they or their family members may resist the ventilator's removal. Economic concerns (sometimes conflicting among family members) come into play

---

[20]See Michael Useem, "Corporate Restructuring and Liberal Learning," *Liberal Education* 81, no. 1 (1995): 18-23.

[21]See Lynton, "New Concepts of Professional Expertise," and McDowell, "Increasing the Liberal Arts Content of Professional/Technical Curriculum" for further discussion of this need.

[22]Lynton, "New Concepts of Professional Expertise," 13.

as costs escalate due to the use of these expensive machines. Furthermore, in some areas of the country, the ventilator may be needed for another more acutely ill patient. If there were a shortage of ventilators, would a 20-year-old patient be given priority over an 80-year-old patient? Liberal studies, applied to real professional dilemmas, may help the professional decide what is moral and ethical, what is "the right thing to do" in such complex situations.

To address these competing factors, critical thinking and higher order reasoning are valued for professional competency. Successful practitioners are required to combine their technical knowledge and skills with an understanding of social and human affairs.[23] We must teach students ways to approach complex problems which are directly related to their professional activity, and to develop the "habit of the mind to deal with complexity . . . central to any definition of the liberally educated person."[24] Both the liberal arts and the professional schools occasionally fail to advance such learning. Neither can blame the other.

As faculty who teach in the professional fields, we value the role of liberal studies in the preparation of competent professional practitioners. In a study of 2,230 professional-field educators at 346 colleges, the faculty members agreed that an educated professional requires four aspects of knowledge specific to their chosen field: (1) conceptual understanding of theoretical foundations; (2) technical skills; (3) the ability to integrate theory with practice; and (4) career marketability.[25] In addition, ten competencies exemplify outcomes that professional education has in common with liberal education. Prominent among these are communication skills, critical thinking, understanding the larger societal context, aesthetic sensibility, professional ethics, leadership capacity, scholarly concern for improvement of the profession, and motivation for continued learning.[26]

The standards proposed through our professional organizational and accrediting bodies increasingly require these competencies in addition to the knowledge specific to the professional field. Accreditation standards

---

[23]Martin H. Krieger, "Broadening Professional Education on the Margins and Between the Niches," *Liberal Education* 76, no. 2 (1990): 6-10.

[24]Lynton, "New Concepts of Professional Expertise," 15.

[25]Stark and Lowther, *Strengthening the Ties That Bind*, 21.

[26]Ibid., 23-25.

set forth by AACSB—The International Association for Management Education—demand that "the general education component for business students should be consistent with the general education required of all students at the institution and should reflect the institution's mission."[27] Specifically, AACSB states that curricular content should include ethical and global issues; the influence of political, social, legal and regulatory, environmental, and technological issues; the impact of demographic diversity on organizations; and written and oral communication.[28]

Other groups continue this theme by proposing similar requirements. For example, the America Association of Colleges of Nursing lists critical thinking, communication, human valuing, ethical reasoning, global health care perspectives, and the application of the social and physical sciences to patient care as necessary skills for professional practice.[29] In its published standards for teacher preparation, the state of California specifies that teacher education should include the following key elements: developing cultural understanding, seeing interdisciplinary connections, using multilingual skills, and "developing self-directed learners who are able to demonstrate, articulate and evaluate."[30] Again, organizations recognize that competent professional practitioners need an understanding of social and human affairs gained through a liberal education alongside the professional knowledge specific to their field.

In addition to enhancing professional outcomes and competencies, liberal studies also give value and meaning to professional education. Ernest L. Boyer proposes the *enriched major* as the "centerpiece of undergraduate education."[31] He adds that an enriched major encourages the students to explore a field in depth and to place their specialty in greater perspective. All majors, including professional majors, should confront three questions:

---

[27]*Achieving Quality and Continuous Improvement through Self-Evaluation and Peer Review* (St. Louis, MO: AACSB—The International Association for Management Education, 1994-95), 17.

[28]Ibid.

[29]*Essentials of Baccalaureate Education for Professional Nursing,* draft copy (Washington, D.C.: American Association of Colleges of Nursing, June 1997).

[30]*California Standards for the Teaching Profession: A Description of Professional Practice for California Teachers* (Sacramento, CA: State of California, July 1997), 5.

[31]Boyer, *College*, 110.

1. What is the history and tradition of the field to be examined?
2. What are the social and economic implications to be understood?
3. What are the ethical and moral issues to be confronted?[32]

To address these questions, a study of our heritage, social institutions, cultural perspectives, economics, and ethical and moral issues again necessitates the integration of liberal and professional education. As so aptly stated by Peter Marsh: "No discipline or profession can be rightly grasped without appreciating its embeddedness in the larger world."[33]

We must also recognize that the professions contribute to liberal studies by bringing "real world" experiences to the classroom. By sharing relevant cases from actual practice, professional students offer a real-life perspective of the non-university environment—thus fostering an understanding of social and human affairs.[34] What student would not have an increased interest in the social, political, and economic causes of poverty after teaching impoverished children or caring for homeless families? What student would not enter into a discussion of the ethical and moral aspects of these same situations after listening to students relate their experiences first-hand? In addition to the need for real-life learning for our traditional students, older adult students returning to college increasingly expect that their studies will be relevant to their ongoing or future employment and/or promotion.[35] Rather than viewing the professional majors and liberal education as competitors, each is an essential component and contributor to a baccalaureate education.

---

[32]Ibid.

[33]Peter T. Marsh, *Connecting the Boundaries of Liberal and Professional Education: The Syracuse Experiment* (Syracuse, NY: Syracuse University Press, 1988), 3.

[34]See Stark and Lowther, *Strengthening the Ties That Bind.*

[35]Robert H. Conn, "Rear Guard on the Escalator: The Struggle to Protect the Liberal Arts Core in Higher Education," occasional papers, no. 80 (Nashville, TN: Board of Higher Education and Ministry, The United Methodist Church, October 1989).

The Christian College, Liberal Arts, and Professional Education

In Christian higher education, liberal studies that integrate Christian beliefs and ethical values with professional education enrich the major and serve as the core of professional studies. In fact, we believe the Christian perspective is one of the strongest links between liberal and professional education. To us, the Christian college is designed to integrate Christian faith with learning and scholarship to equip persons for Christian leadership. As David Baird notes,

> In such an institution, all of life is studied for the discovery of divine truth; and the Christian worldview permeates the totality of college life, including curriculum, co-curriculum, and faculty scholarship. The quest for transcendent truth both in and out of the classroom brings coherence and wholeness to a student's course of study.[36]

Practitioners of nursing, physical therapy, education, social work, computer science, business, and so forth, frequently face questions and make decisions based on an ethical, moral, and theological understanding. Teachers ask, "Are there certain kinds of students in a classroom who are systematically ignored?"[37] Corporate executives ask, "Does this corporate buy-out benefit the greater economy for the business or job security for the employees?"[38] Health care professionals ask, "Are there hospitalized patients with certain diagnoses who receive less attention and nursing care?" Through the professional's relationship with the patient, the client, the consumer, or the student, issues are addressed regarding one's ethical professional conduct and how one ultimately follows God's moral laws.[39]

---

[36]Baird, et al., "Opportunities for Liberal Learning in the Twenty-First Century," 15.

[37]Linda Valli, "Teaching Moral Reflection: Thoughts on the Liberal Preparation of Teachers" (paper presented at the National Forum of the Association of Independent Liberal Arts Colleges for Teacher Education, Milwaukee, Wisconsin, November 1990).

[38]Conn, *Rear Guard on the Escalator*, 6.

[39]George Marsden, *The Outrageous Idea of Christian Scholarship* (New York, NY: Oxford University Press, 1997).

Both individuals and society are affected by such decisions as prolonging life mechanically, caring for the weak and homeless, and guaranteeing equal access to educational opportunities, health care, and social services. Again, one's professional expertise in these decisions requires an informed ethical, moral, and theological foundation. "The university, for all of its concern about the intellect, must never lose sight of the ethical imperative by which it should be guided."[40] If one of the purposes of liberal education is to equip students to serve, then professional education uniquely empowers them to serve a fundamental aim of the Christian's life. If Jesus is the head of all things, then He is head of the professional schools as well as the liberal arts programs.[41]

An interesting illustration of our argument is found in the writings of C. S. Lewis.[42] An educator by profession, Lewis analyzes the moral acceptability of his profession. He concludes,

> Provided, then, that there was a demand for culture, and that culture was not actually deleterious, I concluded that I was justified in making my living by supplying that demand—and that all others in my position (dons, schoolmasters, professional authors, critics, reviewers) were similarly justified; especially if, like me, they had few or no talents for any other career—if their "vocation" to a cultural profession consisted in the brute fact of not being fit for anything else.[43]

The above reference to supply and demand is tantalizing and helps validate those who are educated in and by professional schools. In his own situation, Lewis does not assume teaching literature is a moral good, though he eventually finds some measure of good in it. Then Lewis provides this thought: "The work of the charwoman and the work of the poet become spiritual in the same way and on the same condition. . . . Let us stop giving ourselves airs."[44] We in the professional schools

---

[40]Charles E. Glassick, Mary Taylor Huber, and Gene I. Maeroff, *Scholarship Assessed: Evaluation of the Professoriate* (San Francisco, CA: Jossey-Bass, 1997), 67.

[41]Colossians 1:18.

[42]We are indebted to our colleague William B. McCarty for providing the C. S. Lewis materials and their possible interpretation.

[43]C. S. Lewis, "Christianity and Culture," in *Christian Reflections* (Grand Rapids, MI: Eerdmans, 1994), 20.

[44]Ibid., 24.

wonder if our liberal arts colleagues would agree to substitute "business manager" for "charwoman"? Or, as Lewis' exhortation suggests, is pride the primary cause of the schism between our disciplines?

We conclude that liberal studies are an integral and a greatly needed core for professional education at the baccalaureate level. To prepare professionals for the future, faculty must work together to fashion a curriculum which prepares students for the complexities of tomorrow's world. Rather than a "lamentable chasm" separating the liberal arts college and the professional schools, faculty in both disciplines must practice collaboration, communication, and mutual respect to provide the foundation for future competent practitioners.[45]

Achieving Integration: A Challenge

Herbert Simon argues for a lively integration, an ongoing process importing and exporting ideas from one intellectual discipline to another. He concludes,

> The proper study of mankind has been said to be man. But I have argued that man . . . may be relatively simple, that most of the complexity of his behavior may be drawn from man's . . . search for good designs. If I have made my case, then we can conclude that, in large part, the proper study of mankind is the science of design, not only as the professional component of a technical education but as a core discipline for every liberally educated person.[46]

Such a vision raises several key questions: How might a university develop strategies for bridging the perceived distance between the professional schools and liberal arts? Is it really possible to reintegrate knowledge and learning between the disciplines? Do we have the motivation and wherewithal to refocus and combine our educational efforts to fully make the transition to the information age? Who are the "Great Straddlers" who will make this happen?[47]

---

[45]Stark and Lowther, *Strengthening the Ties That Bind*, 35.

[46]Herbert A. Simon, *The Sciences of the Artificial* (Cambridge, MA: MIT Press, 1969), 159.

[47]Sample, "The Great Straddlers—Successors to the Renaissance Man," 54-57.

There are many specific ways that a Christian university might nurture and encourage the importing and exporting of knowledge between professional schools and liberal studies. We would like to propose the following:

1. Promote faculty participation in interdisciplinary research and/or creative activity.
2. Facilitate interdisciplinary teaching (e.g., team teaching a course with a non-departmental colleague) in order to avoid fragmentation of disciplines.
3. Encourage our best undergraduates to pursue two majors, or at least a major and a minor, in widely separated fields of study.[48]
4. Alter the contexts in which people view knowledge and offset the inclination to split knowledge into ever more esoteric bits and pieces.[49]
5. Collaborate with other departments in development of curricula and instructional materials.
6. Collaborate with the student affairs office for student mentoring, discipling, and advising.
7. Provide opportunities for campuswide dialog (e.g., forums) among liberal arts departments and professional schools.

There need be no chasm between our disciplines. It is time for us to step forward, accept our responsibility, and bridge the gap between disciplines with new strategies, vision, and motivation. It is time for a new wind to blow across the face of the university, resulting in a new model that will educate students not only how to live, but also how to make a living. It is time for those of us who work at Christian colleges to pray that God begin a work at our institutions to break down walls, heal wounds, and energize ministry. It is time for liberal arts and professional faculty to share the responsibility for integrating their two areas.

---

[48]Ibid., 57.

[49]Glassick, Huber, and Maeroff, *Scholarship Assessed*, 9.

Re-Imagining a Distinctively Christian Liberal Arts Education

by Richard Slimbach

Not long ago, I began teaching a course in applied anthropology by asking my students a simple question: "If you did not have to worry about making a living, what would you most like to do for the rest of your life?" I am not sure what I expected, but I was not ready for what I heard. Virtually all of the students dreamed of occupying their lives with travel and sports activities. Not one mentioned anything even remotely related to service to others, much less service among the least, the last, and the lost. Mind you, these were not students enrolled in a state university. They represented the present generation of evangelical college students. While I too love sports activities (I ride my bike to work nearly every day) and am regularly accused of wanderlust, their responses startled me. I came to class assuming a common passion for cross-cultural

---

RICHARD SLIMBACH is professor of global studies and chair of the Department of Global Studies and Sociology at Azusa Pacific University. He is a graduate of Humbolt State University (B.A.), William Carey International University (M.A.), and University of California, Los Angeles (Ph.D.).

understanding and service. When class dismissed, I was left asking myself: Is there anything really distinctive about a Christian college education?

Months later, as I continue to reflect on that class of anthropology students, I wonder if the students' "pre-text" (what they bring to their college experience) is at least as important as the combined affects of their "context" (the institutional environment) and, more particularly, their "text" (the disciplinary content and pedagogical process of the liberal arts). This essay attempts a tentative exploration of these relationships. On a surface level, I hope to offer a set of seven "imaginings" as a series of cognitive signals for rethinking the potential power of a Christian liberal arts education. On a deeper level, however, I am venturing a personal response to the central challenge expressed that day through my class: How might Christian higher education be re-imagined to enable a new generation of Christians to become salt, light, and leaven in all areas of life?[1]

Educating a Post-Christian Generation

After years of interaction with Christian college students, I find much that I admire in them. Generally speaking, they are considerate, polite, and curious. With the overwhelming majority coming from concerned Christian families, they possess strong moral sensibilities, enjoy asking spiritual and ethical questions, and manifest a genuine respect for Jesus Christ. Many will defend the social values of gender equality, multicultural harmony, and environmental stewardship. Consistent with the spirit of adventure expressed among my anthropology students, they are characteristically laid-back, hip and outdoorsy in a Doc Martens, Land's Endish kind of way. That's on a good day. On a bad day, however, informality turns to self-containment, curiosity to conservatism, and the quest to explore and discover to intellectual timidity. They are generally impatient with real ideas and in flight from the unbearable (and seemingly unintelligible) realities closing in upon them. They find it easier to blend

---

[1]This essay explores a variety of issues related to the mission of Christian higher education in an intentionally provocative, and at times confrontational, manner. The author invites reader reactions and the continued exchange of ideas through correspondence (APU, 901 E. Alosta Ave., Azusa, CA 91702) or email (slimbach@apu.edu).

in, to avoid the specter of the "uncool," to not take things too seriously and, above all, to not buck the system that promises to protect their privileged status following graduation. A growing number are disaffected from the Church (many for good reasons) and have been conditioned to expect that religious ideas and institutions belong to the soft, private world of values and opinions and not to the serious, public world of facts. They are the Christian college's first genuinely post-Christian generation.[2]

True to the cool consumerism promoted throughout the general culture, this generation often calculates its present academic investments in terms of their future monetary yield—period. A college education is perceived as the gateway—indeed, the *only* gateway—to a financially secure future. Admissions personnel and faculty advisors encounter an almost intractable what-can-I-do-with-it vocationalism among incoming students. More often than not, the institutions themselves are complicit with this utterly pragmatic outlook. In the struggle to survive the fierce competition for students, many have scaled back or completely abandoned their historic liberal arts mission in order to expand their offerings in specialized and professional subjects that are in greater demand.[3] This is simply one way institutions adapt to an escalating cost-benefit careerism among students and their parents, many of whom question what a broad curriculum in the arts and sciences has to do with real life.

But students are not entirely to blame. As good Americans, they have learned how to live by the rules of consumer capitalism, that "immense cosmos into which the individual is born, and which presents itself to him . . . as an unalterable order of things in which he must live."[4] Education—even a Christian education—readily becomes just another commodity to be used and used up, not unlike a pair of Nike's or

---

[2]Lesslie Newbigin adds this provocative clarification: "[Ours is not,] as we once imagined, a secular society. It is a pagan society, and its paganism, having been born out of the rejection of Christianity, is far more resistant to the gospel than the pre-Christian paganism with which cross-cultural missions have been familiar. Here, surely, is the most challenging missionary frontier of our time." *Foolishness to the Greeks: The Gospel and Western Culture* (Grand Rapids, MI: Eerdmans, 1986), 20.

[3]See David Breneman, *Liberal Arts Colleges: Thriving, Surviving, or Endangered?* (Washington, D.C.: Brookings, 1994).

[4]Max Weber, *The Protestant Ethic and the Spirit of Capitalism* (New York, NY: Charles Scribner, 1958), 54.

a Blockbuster video. Especially within an enculturation system where God has been moved to the periphery or else made into a religious plaything, the central purpose for Christian higher education gets muddled in their (and their parents') minds. Why *does* the Christian college exist? To protect young people against the sin and secularity of public institutions? To offer a good education laced with biblical studies in a morally regulated environment? To cultivate religious commitment among the uncertain? To help one find a Christian life partner? To have the time of one's life while becoming more competitive in the marketplace?[5]

Many parents nevertheless saddle the Christian college with these off-center expectations. As an *in loco parentis* extension of the family, they expect that the Christian college will reinforce, rather than challenge, what some students refer to as a "sweet and sheltered existence." To the extent that faculty and administration are not gripped by higher purposes themselves, or operate in fear of not satisfying their customers, these expectations tend to become normative in the culture of the institution. Students learn to be good, to enjoy a pocket God, to earn high GPAs, to avoid controversy, to vote Republican, to have fun, to take few risks and, above all, to get ahead. A generation ago, courses had to somehow relate to critical social problems; now they only have to relate to one's career. Among a typical graduating class, precious few will be energized by Kingdom ideals or a holy discontent over things as they are. The vast majority will reach commencement as Protestants with nothing to protest, having failed to break through the pale security offered by a cultural Christianity identified with "the American Way of Life."

Inheriting a New Earth

As this generation of Christian collegians leaves the twentieth century, they will enter a world with two faces. In his haunting article entitled

---

[5]Judging from their promotional materials and advertisements, an outside observer would have to conclude that the undergraduate experience at many Christian colleges exists as something between a glorified church camp and a retirement spread for young adults. For prospective customers of graduate programs, the university portrays itself as a flexible and efficient means of enhancing one's marketability. Only occasionally are the academic purposes (for undergraduates) and distinctive Christian identity (for graduate students) of the institution represented. In a buyer's market, they simply do not "sell."

"The Coming Anarchy," Robert Kaplan quotes foreign policy analyst Thomas Fraser Homer-Dixon to describe the cruelly divided world emerging before us:

> Think of a stretch limo in the potholed streets of New York City, where homeless beggars live. Inside the limo are the air-conditioned post-industrial regions of North America, Europe, the emerging Pacific Rim, and a few other isolated places, with their trade summitry and computer-information highways. Outside is the rest of mankind, going in a completely different direction.[6]

Accustomed to life "within the limo," this generation of Christian college students has rarely stopped to ponder those "outside"—the ones who occupy a nightmarish world of disease, filth, malnutrition, unemployment, illiteracy, ethnic strife, fatalism, pain, and sudden death. These conditions have assumed human faces for me. I worked on this essay while residing in Central America where I was reminded daily of the tens of thousands of economically stagnant peasants jammed in huts without electricity or plumbing, forced to sell their labor to landowners who live behind the fortified walls of houses filled with imported entertainment centers and fine furnishings. And the swelling number of children roaming the night streets, hopelessly undernourished, illiterate, and condemned to a life of promiscuity and crime.

But the poverty is not just economic, nor limited to those stuck in the past. In cities like San José and San Salvador, middle-class teenagers are surrendering their cultural identities and values at an alarming rate. They act and look much like their counterparts in Miami or Los Angeles, listening to the same music, watching the same movies, wearing the same clothes, eating many of the same foods, using the same appliances, living in the same kind of houses, attending the same kind of schools, and, of course, learning to speak the same language—English. Neighborhoods which used to nourish local community spirit can no longer compete with the lure of the modern and translocal, whether it be at the ubiquitous McDonald's, in the temple-like mall in city center, or in front of the television which nourishes a commodity consciousness for

---

[6]See Robert Kaplan, "The Coming Anarchy," *The Atlantic Monthly* (February 1994), 44-76.

hours each evening. Each promises a way into the limo—its exotic lifestyles, its power, its identification with a global elite. All they ask is that users be willing to deny their differentiated selves, pick up a standardized monoculture, and follow the all-beneficent processes of globalization. This appears to be the "religion" that is winning the heart of the global teenager.

Imagining a New Liberal Arts

The student "pre-text" and global "context" raises searching questions regarding the "text" of a Christian liberal arts education: What is the relationship of the Christian college, both to its post-Christian children of privilege and to the disprivileged world inhabited by two-thirds of the human family? What biblically informed vision of the "good society" will it take sides with and promote throughout its institutional life? How will we hope, as a community of faith and learning, to imagine, order, and shape the presence of the Kingdom of God in the world? Into what set of understandings, values, relationships, and life commitments will we lead the students in our care? Finally, how will we do it? What kind of college experiences—in and out of class—will provide optimal conditions for equipping our graduates with the competencies needed to fulfill their part in the mission of God? It is in response to these questions that the Christian college will be able to reactivate its mission and redefine the purpose of a liberal education. The discussion that follows begins that process. It invites us to release our God-given capacity to wonder and dream as we re-imagine the core qualities of a distinctively Christian liberal arts education.

1. Imagine the Christian liberal arts as *celebratory*. Colleges and universities that identify themselves as Christian embody a living tradition and a vibrant, celebrated faith. They are grounded in and guided by a convictional framework within which they aim to educate students to live a life of faith—a radically Christian life in contemporary society. As such, a Christian education cannot be, nor pretend to be, all things to all persons. Other schools may consider that the academic enterprise should be carried out in a value-neutral, all-inclusive, non-authoritative, and disinterested manner.[7] This is clearly impossible for the Christian college. It recognizes the fact that value-neutrality is not itself "value-neutral," nor the representation of opinion ever disinterested. Nobody (as postmodernists remind us) can be completely objective and impartial; every academic institution carries a perspective, a fixed starting point, a frame of reference which guides them in matters as diverse as hiring faculty, setting curricular priorities, interpreting research, and defining excellence. The question is not *whether* higher education will promote certain values, but rather *which* values they will be.

This said, the Christian liberal arts will not merely articulate a particular point of view, but celebrate it openly, explicitly, and unapologetically. This is to be done, not in a spirit of propaganda or indoctrination, but in a manner that joins a fair presentation of competing perspectives to a particular witness of faith. But there is no way of avoiding the authority question: if God exists and has spoken, then that speaking must be seen as critically important to ultimate and basic questions of life, meaning, and destiny which reside at the heart of a liberal education. The educational aim becomes not so much to *instruct* students in certain beliefs about Jesus as it is to *incline* them to be a certain type of person—one whose mind, motives, and feelings are permeated with the love and truth of God.

Such a project will require that the Christian college both accept a set of Christian convictions (about human nature, God, Christ, the natural environment, redemption, and eschatology) and apply them throughout the entire institution. This is not a simple task! But it stands reiteration that the college does not automatically become Christian by formulating a clear statement of faith, offering regular chapel experiences, or establishing Bible requirements, though all of these may be important. The much more difficult pursuit will be to charge the entire atmosphere of the school with the consciousness of Christ which, when authentic, produces singleness of purpose, integrity of learning, and a deepened sense of responsibility to the world.

---

[7]The underlying assumption of those who promote a value-neutral approach is that empirical knowledge—the world of facts—bears no intrinsic relationship to the world of spiritual, moral, or social values. Thus, value judgments are merely subjective and self-interested expressions of personal feelings and attitudes.

2. Imagine the Christian liberal arts as *visionary*. Considered from a Christian perspective, the college degree is not a ticket to self-advancement, but an indication of abilities to seek, cultivate, and sustain God's vision of the future. That vision finds its ground in God's self-revelation and dares not be identified either with the alleged triumph of free market capitalism and liberal democracy, or with personal lifestyles showcasing bourgeois values and conspicuous consumption. Rather, its signs are to be found in the evidences of the "now but not yet" Kingdom where the hungry are fed and the naked clothed, where the lives of the unborn and elderly are protected, where basic human rights are defended, where the earth is cared for, and where the gospel is welcomed as "good news" among all peoples. In liberal learning that is eschatologically real, students study and serve in the light of the day when, in real history, God will reconcile all things in heaven and earth (Col. 1:20), liberate all of creation from its bondage (Rom. 8:19-21), sum up all things in Christ (Eph. 1:10), and create a true city where there will no longer be any death, crying, or pain (Rev. 21:4). In this vision of the End, God is "making all things new" (Rev. 21:5)—all of creation is being renewed to a state of ecological harmony and multicultural unity, in which "all the glory and honor of the nations" is made visible, tangible, and audible to all (Rev. 21:24-26).

This is not merely the stuff of religious faith. As Rene Padilla reminds us, "To speak of the Kingdom of God is to speak of God's redemptive purpose for the whole of creation and of the historical vocation that the church has with regard to that purpose here and now."[8] As the educational arm of the Church, Christian higher education shares in that vocation. It looks to eschatology to orient pedagogy—to inform its goals and direct its content and process. It is not enough that we casually assent to the proposition that the overarching purpose of higher education is to develop and assess student talent. The question is, develop that talent toward what desired ends? In short, what kind of person is to be nurtured by what kind of university for what kind of society? In sustained reflection upon this single question, faculty, administrators, and trustees could go far towards re-envisioning the meaning and purpose of a liberal education.[9]

---

[8]Rene Padilla, *Mission Between the Times* (Grand Rapids, MI: Eerdmans, 1985), 186.

[9]A helpful model of this process is provided in the booklet *Liberal Learning at Alverno College*, 5th ed. (Milwaukee, WI: Alverno Productions, 1992).

A distinctively Christian education, in its anticipation of the End, will give less consideration to what students will come *into* the school with than to the dispositions, knowledges, values, virtues, sympathies, skills, and commitments that will characterize them when they go *out*. Working backwards in this way will discipline the subtle drift toward making institutional decisions with only an accountant's pencil. It challenges the college to be driven by serious reflection on God's ultimate intentions rather than, like many of its secular counterparts, simply by an analysis of market trends. In the process, the heart of a Christian liberal arts education is clarified: to provide optimal conditions for *igniting the spirit* to imagine, to wonder, and to worship; for *instructing the mind* to reflect, to ask unasked questions, and to see things in relationship; for *impassioning the heart* to interpret the present, to make value judgments, and to articulate what it loves and hopes for; and for *committing the will* to rebel against false ways of seeing and doing things and to act responsibly and joyfully on behalf of God's vision for the world. In pursuit of these ideals, students learn to image their Creator who reasons with us, seeks to realize the values invested in the creation, and is creatively acting through the sacrificial service of the Church to manifest the Kingdom as historical reality.

3. Imagine the Christian liberal arts as *communal*. The life of faith is not a solitary one; it is lived within a community of believers whose interpersonal relations form around shared practices, obligations, and convictions in pursuit of a common task. For the Christian college, this requires much more than organizing the right curriculum, creating warm fuzzy feelings, enjoying extracurricular activities, or accumulating credits. Rather, it is concerned with fashioning a learning community with the purpose of equipping women and men with the requisite competence to reform individual lives and redirect social institutions as diplomats, business persons, teachers, artists, scientists, nurses, and the like.

While this is our hope, critics of the Church are quick to remind us that mainstream evangelical institutions have historically functioned to reinforce, not redirect, the social status quo.[10] To a large extent, they are

---

[10]They remind us that in different periods of its two thousand year history, the teaching and practice of most Christian churches has condoned slavery, theologically justified racial segregation and anti-Semitism, and in the twentieth century, excluded

correct: radical truth in biblical and Christian history has been preserved more on the critical edges of Christendom than in its mainstream. In oftentimes sacrificial ways, Christian "fringe" movements challenged unjust structures and proclaimed a millennial vision of social equality.[11] They will probably be remembered best for their nonconformity and unpredictability. Their fidelity to the gospel set them against established hierarchies and predictable stances. Admitting that they were "aliens and sojourners on earth. . . . [with] citizenship in heaven" (Heb. 11:13; Phil. 3:20), they knew they could not be molded simultaneously by Jesus and by a particular national or ideological allegiance. To the contrary, in penetrating ways each sought to recapture and offer to the world alternative visions to both the dominant political agenda and the accommodating patterns of the institutional Church. The only label they were free to wear was that of "Christian."

In continuity with this rich evangelical heritage, the contemporary Christian college should be anything but culturally conformist or ideologically predictable. Regrettably, this is rarely the case. Too many Christian colleges have accommodated themselves to the middle-class North American subculture, one which has traditionally existed in such close relationship with Christianity that it has been difficult to distinguish what is American from what is Christian. Under these conditions, Christian education easily degenerates into little more than social respectability and belief in "the American Way of Life." Os Guinness sounds a poignant warning:

> To the extent that well-meaning Christian conservatives (and their institutions) continue to confuse Christian principles and conservative politics, romanticize American history, idolize political power, rely

---

women from ordained ministry and public preaching. In actuality, the evidence is contradictory. For example, it was an evangelical college (Oberlin in New York) that was the first coeducational college in the world, while Wheaton College served as a way station for the underground railroad.

[11]These "Jesus movements" would include the early Benedictines and Franciscans; the sixteenth century Anabaptists and radical reformers; the eighteenth century Moravians and Wesleyans; the nineteenth century Quakers, Mennonites, and Salvation Army; and, in the twentieth century, the historic black churches, the Confessing Church of Nazi Germany, and the "base communities" of Latin America.

> too heavily on single-issue politics, and forget the blistering biblical critique of "religion" . . . the Christian faith is again turned into an ideology in its purest religious form, with the spiritual ideals of the faith serving as weapons for the social interests of the nation.[12]

The necessary first step to reversing this "ideological captivity" is for Christian higher education to reclaim as its overarching purpose the deliberate fashioning of learning communities which will think and act out of alternative values and priorities. Imagine what such a community might look like:

- As a *community of discipleship*, students would be attracted to the Christian college, not as a safe haven where all issues are settled and all truth known, but as a training ground to think for oneself, to disturb old certainties, and to try on new ways of thinking and acting.
- As a *community of reconciliation*, the college community would recruit a multi-ethnic staff and student body to promote the interchange of diverse experiences and perspectives—across ideological, racial, cultural, and social class differences—and provide for a richer exploration of truth.
- As a *community of authenticity*, the various members (administration, staff, faculty, and students) would face problems together, admit and correct mistakes, refuse to hold private agendas, and share decision-making power in a common quest to live out a Kingdom consciousness.
- As a *community of worship*, the chapel service would become central to the educational task of the college. Rather than a fifty-minute spiritual/emotional interlude among otherwise intellectual or social activities, it would be organized to constantly renew the collective Christian mind (and not just arouse feeling), to examine critical academic issues through the eyes of faith (beyond pietistic sermonizing), and to give

---

[12]Os Guinness, *The American Hour: A Time of Reckoning and the Once and Future Role of Faith* (New York, NY: Free Press, 1994), 379.

public expression to the private exercise of spiritual disciplines.[13]

- As a *community of service*, the worship of the head and heart would find expression in the worship of the hands in community service. New students would experience the campus, not as an insular bubble, but as a community at work in integrating theoretical knowledge with first-hand experience dealing with real problems.

4. Imagine the Christian liberal arts as *interdisciplinary*. God is the Creator of all things in heaven and on earth; therefore, all of creation has intrinsic value and integrity and is worthy of serious study—indeed, of conscientious care and protection as the work of God's wise and loving hand. It follows that a liberal arts education from a Christian perspective will *include* representatives from a wide variety of disciplines in celebration of the extraordinary diversity of God's creative acts. It will also *exhibit* the breadth of human thought, culture, and experience in its epistemic relationship to the existence of the Creator, Healer, and Judge of all life. But then it will go one step further, enabling students to *make connections* between disciplinary perspectives on key intellectual and moral issues in order to learn and follow wisdom.

The modern evangelical college has done a poor job with the third imperative. We rarely expect that each course will complement all others like pieces of a puzzle, or that students will be able to see larger trends, patterns, and relationships at the end of their educational journey.[14] There are numerous causes for this, but chief among them is a structural one: We have sub-divided the curriculum into fragments called disciplines and departments, each of which deals with only a small piece of the total picture. This seems to function well *until* we want our students to make

---

[13]There are certain spiritual disciplines which, when absent from the lives of faculty, administration, staff, and students, will all but guarantee that a Christian college will not be able to nurture a distinctively Christian liberal arts education. Here I speak of the habits of solitude, silence, prayerful meditation on Scripture, fasting, and public service.

[14]As an effort in this direction, many schools have incorporated an "integrative seminar" during the senior year. While a step in the right direction, such seminars typically suffer from not enough time to probe disciplinary or ethical relationships in depth.

connections between elements or factors in a whole system (as most of the critical issues on the agenda of Christian mission require). For example, in addressing the issue of globalization, no single discipline will enable students to see the relationships between deforestation and shopping malls, free trade and urban migration, new technologies and street crime, international aid and increased hunger. These are too readily handled as random, disconnected facts and not as threads of a single cloth. Educating students to *think interdisciplinary* means that merely acquainting students with a variety of disciplinary offerings (as is done in the typical general education program) is insufficient. Our central concern should be to help students *unify* their fragments of knowledge into a cohesive, meaningful, and missional vision for life. But this assumes that we, as educators, see that vision clearly ourselves. The reality is that few of us ever stop to consider what kind of student we hope to produce.

As a result, and in the wake of the information explosion of the twentieth century, most Christian educators find it hard to agree on what a liberally educated person should know.[15] "Purists" who categorically reject professional programs in the curriculum as merely "playing to the market" tend to appropriate academic models from pre-Christian Grecian culture. On the other hand, "professionalists" in business, computer science, education, social work, and nursing might be tempted to elevate the importance of the professions over non-professional academic disciplines. They run the risk of reducing God's marvelous works to their market value and the college to a credit factory for fitting students into well-paying jobs.

The eschatological vision discussed earlier compels the content and process of the liberal arts to be referenced to a horizon beyond either the preservation of a particular tradition or the demands of the marketplace. In our mining of God's truth, there can be no complete disjunction between the "liberal" arts and the "useful" arts; indeed, the liberal arts are useful and the useful arts rely on the contributions of the liberal arts. After all, can one hope to understand business without adequate foundations in

---

[15]A century ago, modern history, modern languages, social sciences, and natural sciences were added to the "canon" of the liberal arts. (Thus we now speak of the liberal arts *and* sciences.) Today, some scholars are speaking of technology and ecological design as two of the new "liberal arts" that will again transform the content and process of the liberal arts curriculum.

psychology, sociology, economics, mathematics, and political science? Predictably, an increasing number of students are maneuvering around the formal debates and resistant advisors to combine vital components in professional programs with stock from the traditional liberal arts curriculum. Biology and education majors are learning foreign languages, studying abroad, and pursuing interests in social and political issues. Students in the humanities are selecting minors in business or computer science. Together they are quietly forging a new liberal arts—one that is responsive not only to the wisdom of the ages, but also to the demographic shifts, technical developments, marketplace trends, and intellectual movements of their day.

5. Imagine the Christian liberal arts as *prophetic*. Rather than insulate itself from the contemporary cultural context, the Christian academic community will actively relate to it, both positively and critically. It will be compelled by a transforming vision of life aimed at freeing students from the dominant dispositions and values of the day—e.g., the quest to move upward from weakness to power, from poverty to wealth, from servant to master—in order to illumine the path of Kingdom discipleship. Positively, it will come to understand social reality by engaging in common struggles with community members. Critically, these involvements will compel students to make defensible value judgments based on theologically informed aesthetic, moral, or political values. While this calls upon Christ-followers to take risks in interacting with those persons and ideas which oftentimes belittle religious assumptions and satirize believers, it is essential to the task of expounding a Christian vision of life.

This engagement aims to lead students into an understanding of contemporary thought systems (e.g., naturalism, postmodernism, New Age pantheism) at the level of their core assumptions, discerning and exposing the idolatrous character of "arguments and every pretension that sets itself up against the knowledge of God" (2 Cor. 10:5). At the same time, they will learn to judge the ways in which their own institutions, as households of faith, have been or continue to be complicit with the dominant idols of race, individualism, competition, consumerism, and scientism. Consider for a moment the mad rush on most campuses to "get wired" with the latest information technology. In order to balance the forecasts about how technological innovations will transform the university of the future, we must stop and question the basic premise that the computer is an unqualified social good. It is generally assumed that through email, the Internet, and interactive multimedia, the cybernet will help solve global problems and renew local communities throughout the world. But what of a prophetic critique of the new technologies based on the gospel's call to expose idolatry, overcome oppression, and restore the ecological integrity of the earth? Such a critique would consider how computers are enabling giant financial institutions and multinational corporations to deepen and widen global economic integration; how information exchange under conditions of centralized authority (away from state actors to transnationals) is resulting in downed forests, the displacement of millions of people, the destruction of rural societies, the widespread loss of jobs, the homogenization of cultures, and the promotion of a global consumer ethic; and how microcomputation is altering the pathways of cognition, the ways we learn.[16]

In expecting that the Christian college will give students experience in challenging assumptions and clarifying presuppositions, we are acknowledging that sin not only distorts our ability to *gain* knowledge, but also distorts the *content* and *use* of the knowledge we do gain. Thus, there can be no unconditional acceptance of the claims or insights of our disciplines. It follows that one of the most important goals of a Christian liberal arts education becomes that of cultivating in ourselves and our students a *wise skepticism* towards the received knowledge in our fields, as well as regarding our personal and institutional achievements. Christian educators will lead students into reflecting theologically upon the secular assumptions (e.g., notions of "liberal neutrality," "the autonomous self," and "technical progress") that underlie their field of study. In so doing, they will assume that both the goodness of creation and the fallenness of human nature will in varying degrees find expression in the assumptions, methods of inquiry, models, and conclusions of their disciplines as the context of the larger cosmic warfare over human lives.

---

[16]Granted, I am relying on a computer at this moment to compose this essay with greater ease and speed than could be had with a conventional typewriter. But periodically I stop and wonder: If Jesus enabled me to look back one hundred years from now to assess the impacts of the computer (as we can now in the case of the automobile), what questions concerning computer technology would He want me to ask?

6. Imagine the Christian liberal arts as *integrative*. In contrast to the lack of philosophical and pedagogical coherence and unity characterizing most of higher education, the Christian college continues to affirm that faith commitments, moral feeling, and a comprehensive worldview should properly guide intellectual knowing and responsible action. This conviction underlies the truest attempts to integrate faith and learning. It also suggests, boldly enough, that the humanities and sciences cannot be fully understood and thus stand incomplete apart from the knowledge of God. We dare not affirm this in a cavalier manner, given the lack of theological consensus and intellectual creativity in much of popular evangelicalism. Neither can we fail to remind ourselves that an intellectual mastery of the Scriptures and theology is useless (and even detrimental) unless accompanied both by personal piety and the continuous testing of Christian revelation in public settings. Nevertheless, the theological/spiritual disciplines must be kept pre-eminent among the disciplines in a Christian liberal arts curriculum if there is to be any serious attempt to integrate faith and learning.[17] Christian colleges should be encouraged to experiment with various ways of creatively doing this. Underlying each effort, though, will be the common conviction that a growing knowledge of and commitment to Jesus as Lord should illumine rather than limit our search for truth.

In their pursuit of faith-learning integration at the highest level, those of us in Christian colleges can lose our way in one of two directions. One hazard is to lapse into a purely privatized and intellectually rigid relationship towards the secular world. Academically, this leads the institution to withdraw from mainstream scholarship and to cultivate piety at the expense of learning.[18] A second hazard is to become so

---

[17]Many Christian educators maintain that the integration of faith and learning does not necessarily require that "pure" Bible or theology courses be offered, but that Christian perspectives can be infused throughout the curriculum. They highlight the fact that many Bible courses are caught up in exegetical concerns unrelated to the broader questions and critical issues facing humanity. But the "infusion" model would seem to require that most faculty be able to critique the conceptual assumptions, methods of inquiry, and applications in their discipline from a biblical perspective. How many, in fact, are able to do so?

[18]Many curricular and co-curricular programs sponsored by such schools are educationally counterproductive as a result. For example, unless conducted with the input and under the scrutiny of appropriate disciplinary understandings, students participating in missions outreaches and service projects often lapse into unreflective mindsets and culturally insensitive behaviors. One wonders if many actually end up doing more harm than good.

enamored with achieving public visibility, recognition, and influence that we, as an academic community, come to gauge our success *primarily* in terms of the size of our enrollment, the amount of our endowment, the expanse of our property, the grandeur of our buildings, the literary productivity of our faculty, and the national ranking of our institution. Absolutized, these desirable things become part of the Great Lie that human life can derive its meaning in independence from biblical values that exist in tension, if not conflict, with the values of contemporary society. Schools can be led into this secularizing temptation either from *above* (through decisions made by trustees and senior administrators calculated to achieve institutional respectability on par with their secular counterparts)[19] or from *below* (through faculty who allow such measures of "success" to compensate for feelings of intellectual inferiority). In either case, the end result is a mental and moral assimilation to domesticated forms of education.

The distinctively Christian alternative is to organize education to engage society at the point of its central intellectual questions and concerns. In doing so, it can hope to offer more promising life-views and life-styles than are available through non-Christian systems of thought. This level of faith-learning integration progresses beyond the evidences of caring and integrous professors and required courses in Bible and Church History, beyond statements of faith, chapel services, class prayers, and campus Bible studies. These are all available through other state or church institutions. To genuinely integrate faith and learning in a liberal arts context will require that faculty and students experience their education together as an act of love and worship to God, activating a common quest to reason and respond theologically in relation to issues that cut across multiple disciplines. This kind of "Christian theorizing" is grounded in (a) the ability to demonstrate a Christian lifestyle nurtured through spiritual disciplines; (b) the conceptual knowledge of what the Bible meant in the cultures in which it was revealed and what it means for us in our

---

[19]One trend in much of Christian higher education that I find disturbing is that of hiring senior administrators out of successful professional and business backgrounds, and not from professorial and theological backgrounds. While many are quite competent in managing capital campaigns and important administrative tasks, few can be expected to also have a thorough enough understanding of educational philosophy, classroom pedagogy, and faith integration to lead faculty in these areas and make decisions that properly balance the institution's educational mission with market realities.

cultures; (c) a thorough mastery of one's discipline; (d) the ability to reflect theologically upon the secular content of one's discipline and to evaluate it according to the norms of Jesus and the Kingdom; and (e) a dispositional passion ignited by a great love for life and a commitment to applying academic knowledge to real community problems. This kind of faith-learning integration constitutes the *sine qua non* of a distinctively Christian education.[20]

7. Imagine the Christian liberal arts as *redemptive*. The vision of the Christian liberal arts is not only *of* the world, but also *for* the world. This means that the Christian college, rather than insulate students from the surrounding society, will inculcate in them a sense of mission in it.[21] Liberal learning in a Christian context is expected to have redemptive power in producing students who will unite intellectual integrity and ethical conviction with compassionate involvement as salt and light in the world. But to what extent is that power evident in today's Christian colleges? How many students exhibit a compelling passion for truth and for justice? How many are fired by the missiological significance of their studies? On commencement day, what would a degree from a Christian college or university represent to most students: the necessary first step toward a prosperous career? A symbol of groups joined, tasks accomplished, and friends made? A receipt for knowledge-on-board? Certainly few (myself included) would contest the importance of graduates demonstrating an interdisciplinary breadth of understanding, a sense of history, analytic and critical thinking skills, and the ability to "learn how to learn" throughout one's lifetime. But wouldn't *any* decent college education produce this kind of competence? "Yes," some might argue, "but students in evangelical colleges also form a Christian worldview

---

[20]For an expanded analysis of "Christian theorizing" see George Marsden, *The Outrageous Idea of Christian Scholarship* (New York, NY: Oxford University Press, 1997).

[21]"Mission" is used here to refer to those activities which, by word and deed, and in light of particular conditions and contexts, offer every individual and human institution everywhere a valid opportunity to be challenged to a radical realignment of their affections, attitudes, priorities, and principles of life with those of the Lord Jesus, as something of that reality is made visible, audible, and tangible by the church. See David Bosch, *Transforming Mission: Paradigm Shifts in Theology of Mission* (New York, NY: Orbis Books, 1993), 389-420.

and a greater confidence in the gospel." While we would hope this happens, at least one study claims it is the exception.[22] Even for those for whom it is true, we have to ask whether an intellectual understanding of Christian truth is sufficient. Can we be content with the *discovery* of knowledge without concern for how that knowledge is *applied*?

A Christian liberal arts education focused on nurturing a redemptive faith in students must not be seen as a primarily cognitive and dispassionate endeavor. The critical questions to ask are, What does that faith look like? What is its vision for the world? Is it a faith that is content to *talk about* a Christian worldview in our preparation of scientists, journalists, therapists, educators, and musicians who will, if lucky, achieve an innocuous success within the prevailing order? Or is it a faith that compels each graduate to actively *take sides* with God in building "the new heaven and the new earth"? At a moment in history when nearly a billion members of the human family live at the edge of starvation and the gap between rich and poor is widening virtually everywhere, Christ-followers cannot simply look away.

Nor can they be neutral. The Scriptures clearly reveal Christ as taking sides with the "losers" in the new world order.[23] The question for the Christian liberal arts is not *Shall* it take sides?, but With whom is it *already* siding? Is it enabling students, in the words spoken by Dietrich Bonhoeffer to his privileged friends after ten years of resistance against Hitler, "to see the great events of the world from below, from the perspective of the outcast, the suspects, the maltreated, the powerless, the oppressed, the reviled—in short, the perspective of those who suffer"?[24] Or is it confirming students in perspectives and social positions complicit with an economic, cultural, and political system normed on

---

[22]In a study of Christian liberal arts colleges, James Davison Hunter found that, "whatever religious beliefs and practices an individual carried in with him at the start of his educational sojourn would have been either seriously compromised or abandoned altogether by the time he was ready to graduate." *Evangelicalism: The Coming Generation* (Chicago, IL: University of Chicago Press, 1987), 171.

[23]Numerous passages reveal God's primary and partisan concern for the economic, moral, and spiritual struggles of the poor and marginalized segments of every society. See, for example, Lk. 1:46-53; Lk. 4:16-21; Lk. 6:20-21; Lk. 7:18-23; and Matt. 25:31-46.

[24]Dietrich Bonhoeffer, *Letters and Papers from Prison* (London: SCM Press, 1971), 17.

commercial drive, technological control, racial (white) dominance, and military might? Every curriculum takes a stand in that it reflects an image of a preferred future. Toward what redemptive ends will the Christian liberal arts deliberately guide learning? On what basis will it appraise the social outcomes of students? Beyond the acquisition and critique of knowledge, what ethical commitments will alumni be expected to demonstrate?

Conclusion

This discussion has set forth seven marks of a distinctively Christian liberal arts education. Taken together, they call upon colleges and universities to a deliberate and (seemingly) radical "re-imagining" of their institutional life for producing students who will affect, rather than be affected by, the world of the twenty-first century. They also constitute a clear antidote to the process of what Donald Dayton terms "institutional embourgoisement" that imperceptibly acts to transform Christ-centered schools into irrelevant religious institutions. In our day, that domesticating process has accelerated. The faithfulness of Christian educators is being severely tested by the devaluation of the transcendent world and the deterioration of Christian influence throughout society. We are in danger, not of having plenty of faith without our knowing how to integrate learning into it, but rather too little faith to care how it might reshape a God-emptied world.

In such a crisis, we cannot be content with add-ons and half-measures. By the turn of the century, the distinctiveness of a Christian liberal arts education will not be measured primarily by the standards which rank institutions in the *U.S. News & World Report* "Best Schools" issue, but rather by engagement in teaching-learning that celebrates a vibrant faith, envisions a glorious future, nurtures a Kingdom-centered community, unites the best of liberal and professional learning, examines truth claims at the level of core assumptions, integrates biblical wisdom with disciplinary knowledge, and energizes mission through every sphere of life. If faithful to its mission, Christian higher education will still be accorded minority status by the larger society. But rather than cause for further re-entrenchment, that status will actually provide us with a tremendous opportunity for a re-exhibition of hope. The words of Carl F. H. Henry remind us of the possibilities:

> It is compatible with the God of historical surprises that some secular campus, being chastened and nauseated by the perturbing instability and intellectual nihilism to which postmodernism leads, might through reexploration of the history of thought, venture once again, through its evangelical remnant, to reconsider the Judeo-Christian theistic option and through earnest intellectual activity theoretically acknowledge again its compelling logic and experiential power. To have some modest part in such a conceptual recovery is the opportunity that now overhangs the life of the Christian.[25]

---

[25]Carl F. H. Henry, "The Christian Pursuit of Higher Education," *Faculty Dialogue* 24 (Spring 1995), http://www.iclet.org/pub/facdialogue/24/henry24.

Part Two

ഇശ

The Reviews

The Idea of a University by John Henry Newman

Reviewed by Daniel C. Palm

Arriving in Ireland in 1851, the newly appointed rector of the newly established Catholic University in Dublin found a problem awaiting: a significant portion of the Irish public entertained doubts about the necessity of a distinctly Roman Catholic university. Other religious institutions for the education of young men were readily at hand in mid-nineteenth century Ireland, and they kept the peace by leaving matters of faith aside. The new rector, John Henry Newman, understood the seriousness of the situation: If those who questioned the fledgling university went unanswered, the school might find itself lacking both students and financial support from the community. And so in reply to these doubters, Newman set about in 1852 to deliver a public defense of the new university.[1] The nine essays that he wrote and published as pamphlets that year (five of which were presented to the public as lectures), alongside

---

DANIEL C. PALM is an associate professor of political science in the College of Liberal Arts and Sciences at Azusa Pacific University. He is a graduate of Augustana College (B.A.), University of Chicago (M.A.), and Claremont Graduate School (Ph.D.).

[1]For more on the historical setting of Newman's discourses, see Martha McMackin Garland, "Newman in His Own Day," in Frank Turner, ed., *The Idea of a University* (New Haven, CT: Yale University Press, 1996), 265-281.

ten additional discourses on university subjects he would add in 1873, comprise the work we know as *The Idea of a University*. For the remainder of his life, Newman would continue to revise and edit the work through nine editions, the last published a year before his death in 1889. The book continues to intrigue academicians and all those interested in the nature and mission of universities and liberal education.

Limiting our discussion to the nine original discourses, Newman explains that his project will focus upon the aims and principles of education. And if these things will take some time to expound, Newman is clear from the outset what the university ought *not* produce, namely, one of "the chief evils of the day," a "spurious philosophism" that he describes as "viewiness":

> An intellectual man, as the world now conceives him, is one who is full of "views" on all subjects of philosophy, on all matters of the day. It is almost thought a disgrace not to have a view at a moment's notice on any question from the Personal Advent to the Cholera or Mesmerism. (pp. 9-10)

Lying behind this sad intellectual trend, Newman speculates, is the need to fill the dozens of journals and magazines characteristic of modern democracy in nineteenth century Britain. But to avoid this—to arrive at real truth rather than mere "views"—the student must be trained *how to think*, to gain the proper habits of method, "of making his ground good as he goes," and distinguishing what is known from what is not. If an education of this sort can be accomplished, the student will turn gradually toward "the largest and truest philosophical views, and will feel nothing but impatience and disgust at the random theories and imposing sophistries and dashing paradoxes, which carry away half-formed and superficial intellects" (p. 10).

The nine discourses address three large matters. Discourses I–IV comprise Newman's response to the "intellectual absurdity" of universities that do not provide for the study of theology. Because he considers theology a matter of knowledge as well as faith, he argues that theological inquiry has not only a rightful place within the university, but that an education without a religious component is deficient. Be that as it may, he holds that one might still learn much from the curricula and practices followed in these universities. In the final two discourses, VIII and IX, the author considers the relation between the university and the Roman Church. But it is in the second and central part of the work, Discourses V–VII, that Newman explicitly grapples with the nature of liberal education, and how it might differ from vocational or professional instruction.

Newman begins his discussion of liberal education with the premise that knowledge constitutes a whole, and that the various sciences each address a part of that whole. The university serves as the place where the student can touch some of the parts by "living among those and under those who represent the whole circle." It permits the student to apprehend "the great outlines of knowledge, the principles on which it rests, the scale of its parts, its lights and its shades, its great points and its little, as he otherwise cannot apprehend them." The education one receives there is called "liberal" because it forms a "habit of mind" characterized by freedom, equitableness, calmness, moderation and wisdom (p. 77).[2] Newman reminds the reader that the grammatical opposite to something *liberal* is something *servile*, and that hence a liberal education is the sort of education suitable for a free person.

Of course there exist other sorts of instruction that stand in contrast to liberal education, namely those that concern commerce or one of the professions. Though he has used the word *servile* in this context, Newman is hardly scornful, noting that these forms of education can and often do require the utmost of the intellect. And even those forms of education that demand less—even much less—are still honorable and essential to civilization. Echoing Aristotle's *Rhetoric*, he argues that the other forms of education differ only in their direction. They aim at the acquisition of some skill or other, while liberal education alone is "independent of sequel, expects no complement, refuses to be *informed* (as it is called) by any end, or absorbed into any art, in order duly to present itself to our contemplation" (p. 81). That is to say, a liberal education is not in the service of any other thing; it is undertaken for the sake of knowledge, and knowledge, when we achieve it, is its own reward.

The latter point is central to Newman's argument about liberal education. Humans derive pleasure from learning. We go to great lengths and strive continually to learn, to know those things that we may hope to be able to know. True, few of us have the means, mental capacity, or

---

[2]One is reminded that the word "liberal" derives from the Latin adjective *liber*, meaning "free," and that the word has only recently taken on the weighty political baggage that it now bears.

inclination to indulge in the quest for knowledge all the time, but many of us can devote some of our leisure to it, if only for those few years after we attain maturity but before we sign a job contract or marriage certificate.

Charming as all this may sound, Newman understood that his less prosperous Irish audience—and the advocates of a strictly utilitarian education, many of whom wrote for the *Edinburgh Review*—would remain unsatisfied. They could be expected to press, "What is the *use* of it?" A fair question, since, as Newman admits, a liberal education does not result in secular or material good on the one hand, nor in moral goodness on the other—knowledge does not necessarily make one either rich or good. Nor does it necessarily incline one toward Christianity or Catholicism. Newman's reply is that the end product of a liberal education is another good thing, namely, the gentleman, whom he describes as a person of "cultivated intellect, a delicate taste, a candid, equitable, dispassionate mind, a noble and courteous bearing in the conduct of life" (p. 89).

If his mention of gentlemanship strikes our modern sensibilities as quaint—and who, upon mention of the word, does not momentarily conjure up an image that includes a walking stick and spats?—Newman has an answer. The gentlemanship that emerges from liberal education has nothing to do with class status. It is simply the moderate behavior that characterizes good members of society; it is "fitness for the world" (p. 125). This is a notion that is hardly antiquated, whether put forth by Newman in the nineteenth century, or by his teacher Aristotle in the fourth century B.C.

Newman concludes with a word of warning. Because institutions that teach liberal education regard truth as beautiful, there exists a danger that students will come to think of religious faith as merely another human exercise. Newman does not go so far as to claim that each student undertaking a liberal education can be expected to reject the faith, but that they "will measure and proportion it by an earthly standard" (p. 151). That just this sort of thing will happen to their children as they leave home for college is enough to drive God-fearing parents to distraction. The familiar religious faith learned at home and in church is about to be challenged by a world of new ideas. In response, some Christian faculty, in Newman's day and our own, have severely limited the literature, arts, and sciences that are studied in college courses, including only those that might be called "Christian-friendly." But to this Newman replies, "why do we educate, except to prepare for the world?" A student whose education for the world is "today confined to the Lives of the Saints [will be] tomorrow thrown upon Babel," and woefully unprepared will that young person be. It is only by teaching the classic texts that the young can learn to distinguish "beauty from sin, the truth from the sophistry of nature, what is innocent from what is poison" (p. 161).

Newman's argument about liberal education is made within the context of Roman Catholicism, and includes criticism of Protestantism along the way. Yet one need not be more than a believer of what C. S. Lewis called "mere Christianity" to find intriguing his larger claim that theology has a rightful place within a liberal education. It is the task of the Church, and the study of theology, to inform each part of liberal education with something higher. Literature, the arts, the sciences—each, writes Newman, "has its imperfection, and [the Church] has her remedy for each. She fears no knowledge, but she purifies all; she represses no element of our nature, but cultivates the whole." Far from prohibiting any sort of truth, she ensures "that no doctrines pass under the name of Truth but those which claim it rightfully" (p. 161).

Times have changed. In our age, theology—at one time the discipline that reigned over the social sciences—is unwelcome at the secular university, replaced by departments that approach religion and even biblical literature and theology as mere cultural phenomena. Courses in comparative religion can be found alongside others in comparative politics and comparative dance. The idea that the study of theology might serve as a forum for the consideration of the nature of God or humanity, or the great questions that human beings ask, has been all but banished.

Underlying this problem of theology's rightful place is another reflected in Newman's opening assault on "viewiness." His several discourses argue that, however difficult the task, human beings *can* come to know the truth. In this he is at odds with much if not all of the modern university, whose members take care not to speak of "truths" and have all but forgotten the word "principle." Both words have been replaced by "values," all of which, like "tastes," are created equal, and no one of which has any greater claim to truth than the next. To argue that one set of values might be true, right, or good is to "impose one's value system" on others, and the highest affront. It is no longer thought possible that anything can be known because nothing is thought to be universally true. And so it is that the liberal education of today stands in danger of becoming a mere sampling of views, the very thing that Newman understood as the opposite of liberal education.

The Idea of a University reminds modern-day proponents of true liberal education—an education that regards truth and knowledge as real and within human grasp—that they have a daunting, but by no means impossible, task. As believers in God's truth, Christian scholars and their universities have had that task thrust upon them.

The Higher Learning in America

by Robert Maynard Hutchins

Reviewed by John Culp

In 1936, Robert Hutchins presented an ideal for higher education which continues to challenge practices in higher education today. In the face of the external pressures that faced university education and the internal dilemmas that developed due to its nature, Hutchins proposed a program of "higher learning" solidly based upon general education. The current confusion about higher education both parallels the situation which he faced and indicates the failure of educational institutions to respond to his ideal.

Hutchins' examination of higher education revealed a state of confusion about whether its purpose was to prepare students for life or further education. He identifies three external causes. The first is the pressure to fund the continuation of the institution. Higher education compromises its purpose to prepare students for the life of the mind by attempting to

---

JOHN CULP is professor of philosophy in the C. P. Haggard School of Theology at Azusa Pacific University. He is a graduate of Greenville College (B.A.), Asbury Theological Seminary (M.Div.), Butler University (M.A.), and Claremont Graduate School (Ph.D.).

satisfy a variety of potential sources of funding. The second cause is a misunderstanding of democracy. Democracy requires that every individual be given the *opportunity* for education, not that every individual receive the same amount and type of education. The final source of the confusion characterizing higher education is the erroneous notion that progress in learning is the accumulation of data rather than the pursuit of intellectual virtues and the advancement of knowledge. Understanding progress as nothing more than the accumulation of data eventually culminates in anti-intellectualism.

Internal debates about the purpose of a university intensify the muddle, according to Hutchins. When universities fail to provide a haven for the unhampered search for truth, they face three dilemmas: professionalism, isolation, and anti-intellectualism. Professionalism emphasizes practice rather than reflection about practices. Isolation results from an emphasis upon specialization and destroys the unity of the university. Anti-intellectualism arises out of the desire to provide professional training and frustrates the efforts of the university to educate. Hutchins proposes that the university focus on the pursuit of truth for its own sake in order to resolve these dilemmas.

To guide higher education to greater clarity, Hutchins offers the ideal of education with the purpose of developing human powers more fully. Such an education would consist of general education and "higher learning." General education develops the elements of common human nature by helping the student connect the present to the past, relate person to person, and advance the thinking of humanity. Students need to know a common language, have a general interest in advancing knowledge, and possess a common stock of fundamental ideas. This common intellectual training will enable individuals to interact with fields of learning other than their own. "Higher learning" builds upon general education in order to continue the development of human powers. It involves the student in the fundamental problems of metaphysics as first principles, of social science, and of natural science. Students would take courses with the faculty in each of these three areas but would work in more depth in the area central to their career plans. Technical education, or training, would not occur until the program of higher learning had been completed.

Hutchins draws a clear distinction between general education and what he calls "higher learning." Hutchins does not use this contrast to denigrate vocational preparation, although he is quite clear that university education should not involve specific professional training. Nor does he provide a traditional list of liberal arts courses. Instead, he identifies the primary goal of higher education as the development of human powers, the same goal that is traditionally associated with the liberal arts. This development is actualized by combining general education and "higher learning": general education provides a foundation in the liberal arts, and "higher learning" leads the student into more sophisticated and independent work in the liberal arts. Taken together, these two curricula prepare the person to participate in a democratic society and successfully pursue an occupation.

The commonality of language, thinking skills, and concepts accomplished through general education enables a person to participate in society. In fact, Hutchins states that this type of learning must be available to all members of a society, not just to those who can benefit from higher education. Such a commonality prepares a person for advanced and independent thinking. This helps the individual avoid the dissatisfying limitation of the breadth of human experience which often occurs with specialization. Without this commonality and appreciation for the breadth of human experience, the individual becomes limited to a specific occupation and, ultimately, to a wholly inadequate way of thinking.

Higher education also contributes to society through its relevance to the professions. Education in independent thinking facilitates the development of the professions and occupations by freeing the professional from the limits of the immediate and the past. The person who has developed the ability to think theoretically and broadly will provide insights into the nature and potential of a profession or occupation that those limited to daily practices will be unable to offer. This ability is not divorced from current practice but helps develop more adequate practices.

Hutchins provides helpful resources for reflection about Christian higher education, although there are two limitations of his book in that regard. The first grows out of his optimism of the classical understanding of human existence as rational. Hutchins articulated an understanding of higher education that drew deeply from traditional educational emphases upon the importance of reflection and the development of human rationality. The difficulty in achieving this development among humans who are both rational and irrational must be recognized. However, this classical understanding of human existence as rational is not opposed to a Christian perspective as much as it is a partial insight lacking a trans-human perspective.

The second limitation arises out of Hutchins' context. He recognizes that the context in American education dealt, and continues to deal, with religious differences by excluding religious considerations from public discussion. Because of this context, he calls for a metaphysical rather than a theological principle to guide education. Christian higher education as private rather than public can utilize a theological foundation for education. Such a theological rationale can be constructed on doctrines such as creation and redemption. Creation establishes the basic value of human existence and rationality. Redemption provides the motivation for education as participation in the process of redemption by completing what was begun by divine action.

Hutchins supplies a number of helpful insights for the effort to formulate an ideal Christian higher education based upon theological principles. His analysis of the confusion in higher education as a result of external pressures describes the majority of Christian institutions of higher education. A legitimate concern of Christian higher education has always been to prepare students for life by teaching the religiously accepted understanding of reality. At the same time, Christian higher education has always been at least incipiently aware that the educational process has transcendent elements that often modify the religious tradition which is being propagated. Hutchins' analysis of the external pressures upon higher education can assist Christian higher education in recognizing and identifying those pressures both in relation to the constituency which directly supports it and the broader society. Must Christian institutions only repeat what the constituency has said in the past in an effort to maintain or increase enrollments, or are they led by a principle which recognizes God's prophetic call to every Christian tradition? Does being an institution of Christian higher education mean that only the persons with sufficient financial resources can graduate, or does it mean finding ways to enroll students who are prepared to enter into the human activity of reflection and catch the vision of helping all people reflect about their existence in relation to God, others, and the natural world? Finally, is progress at Christian institutions of higher learning defined only in terms of the number of graduates who maintain a specific theological tradition and ratings in listings of educational institutions, or is progress defined in terms of insights into human existence applied to the individual and social lives of human beings?

Hutchins' discussion of the internal dilemmas faced by institutions of higher education raises similar issues for Christian higher education. Such institutions struggle with what it means to be an educational institution and face the temptation to surrender education to pressures for results and usefulness. Recognizing their parallels to the dilemmas of professionalism, isolation, and anti-intellectualism will help institutions of Christian higher education draw upon the theological resources that can assist them in solving these dilemmas. The theological doctrines of divine omnipotence and omniscience provide a basis for resisting the pressure to prepare students solely for occupations or only for the religious aspect of human existence. The completeness of God's creative activity provides a basis for avoiding the privatization and isolation of religious concerns from the rest of life. The divine gift of rationality and the call to communicate the truth challenges any tendency toward anti-intellectualism.

Hutchins' efforts met immediate criticisms about assuming a monolithic rationality and excluding different understandings of human existence. While Hutchins clearly assumes the importance of human rationality, the contemporary reader must be careful not to presume too much by Hutchins' commitment to human rationality. It is true that both Christian and non-Christian readers will have to carry Hutchins' concern for the development of human existence beyond what he may have understood in terms of cultural and intellectual breadth. It does not follow that Hutchins' ideal has no contribution to that effort. His repudiation of empiricism and vocationalism is not simply the repetition of ancient philosophical systems and canons. It challenges proposals for responses to contemporary concerns by special groups. In so far as those proposals fail to acknowledge the breadth of human existence, they increase and exacerbate the tensions in contemporary culture rather than transforming those tensions into resources for the further development of human existence.

Hutchins contributes most significantly to contemporary reflection about the liberal arts and higher education through his clear articulation of the purpose of higher education as preparation for participation in the life of thought. Although it will be difficult to gain a consensus on exactly what its content will be like today, a shared commitment to the life of thought provides the best alternative to a chaos of different groups. While some of the details of Hutchins' proposal will not be helpful in the present context, education along the lines he proposes has the potential to bring about transformation. Hutchins calls those committed to the life of thought to find new ways in the current context to prepare the next generation.

General Education in a Free Society
and
The Idea and Practice of General Education

Reviewed by Richard Christopherson and David Miyahara

In the accounts offered by the faculties of Harvard College in 1945 and the University of Chicago in 1950, two forces were at work shaping the ideas about general education. First, there was the recognition of a crisis brought about by the demise of religiously based education. The last remnants of genteel Protestantism had been dismantled and a new, more secularized curriculum installed. Second, and compounding the crisis of faith, was the prominence of "specialism" or "departmentalism" in postwar American universities. New ideas about general education were offered in response to the growing influence of pragmatic, discipline-based curriculums.

RICHARD CHRISTOPHERSON is professor of sociology in the College of Liberal Arts and Sciences at Azusa Pacific University. He is a graduate of Wheaton College (B.A.), California State University, Hayward (M.A.), and University of California, Davis (Ph.D.). **DAVID MIYAHARA** is an assistant professor of sociology in the College of Liberal Arts and Sciences at Azusa Pacific University. He is a graduate of University of California, Irvine (B.A.), and Stanford University (M.A., Ph.D.).

A century earlier, American colleges and universities had been united around the central purpose of training the "Christian citizen," and there was a clarity about how to accomplish this: mathematics for logic, the classics for "taste," rhetoric for speech, and Christian ethics for moral values (Harvard, *General Education in a Free Society*, p. 43). As the ideal of the Christian citizen was abandoned, universities were pushed towards professionalism—specialized training for specific vocations. Education became more narrowly defined by a growing number of subfields. The goals of "liberal" education, "that which benefits or helps to make men free" (Harvard, p. 52), and that which "provides the conditions for the pursuit of truth, for freedom of speech and action, and for the flowering of men's creative powers in literature and the arts" (Chicago, *The Idea and Practice of General Education*, p. 7), were being subverted by demands for practical and technical kinds of schooling. The possibility of a generally educated citizenry—wise, capable of realizing their full potential as individuals, bound together in their understanding of a unifying heritage, sharing a common method of inquiry—was in jeopardy. Individuals were increasingly isolated by differences in their specialized training. Emile Durkheim's division of labor had caught up with the American university and threatened to destroy the homogeneous certainty of earlier times.

By mid-twentieth century, the educational legacy was one "of disturbance and maladjustment" as the consensus about the purposes of education had been eroded by unprecedented social change (Harvard, p. 42). How can the center hold now that we have discarded (or privatized) our religious ideals and been swept off our mooring by the impressive accomplishments of specialized scholarship and practice? Universities were faced with questions: What should the "rising generation" be taught? What should Americans be like? How can general education improve our citizenry? What is common to Americans as a people and as a nation, and how can this heritage be institutionalized in the education system? Hopes for restoring order in the academy rested squarely on plans for a reformed general education.

The approach to reform at Harvard College and the University of Chicago is based on a Western, European model of national societies which had been in development since the Reformation. The guiding assumptions are: (1) the primacy of the individual and individual action; (2) the nation as a society made up of individuals; (3) the value of progress; (4) childhood socialization as the key to adult character; and (5) the state as the guardian of the nation.[1] Conspicuously absent from these assumptions is any clear sense of transcendent moral obligation. This set of interrelated beliefs linked the development of children (and young adults) to the national interest. As a result, mass education was seen as not only a nation-building project, but an explicitly secular project as well. From this perspective, education arose as a logical weapon of national defense in America's economic and political competition with other nations. At mid-century, the key issues in this competition were political and dealt with the preservation of democracy in response to the threats posed by fascism and communism, while in the 1980s, the key issues would center on economics and involve the national response to "Japan, Inc."

The task of protecting national interests has two components: the need to unify a diverse citizenry and the need to remain ahead of international competition. This tension drives the "push-pull" between general and specialized education in the nation's colleges. The struggle to invigorate general education at Harvard and Chicago was animated by both the historical urgency of their nation-building agenda, and by the increasing importance of specialized, science-based, professionalized programs in the undergraduate curriculum. They wanted to preserve loyalty to the secularized ideals of the past while making orderly progress into a technologically sophisticated future.

Fifty years ago, it was not especially difficult for the faculties of Harvard and Chicago to envision—and in the case of the University of Chicago, to enact—the sort of general education they felt the nation needed. There was debate, and the systems of education proposed in each book are not identical, but from our late twentieth century perspective, these two accounts are far more alike than different. The faculties shared a certainty about many things: they were certain that the right kind of general education is key to preserving democracy and building a free society. Certain that they did not want to reintroduce religion in general or Judeo-Christian Scripture in particular into the center of university life. Certain that religious faith was unnecessary in the academy because there were other less divisive faiths to adopt—faith in reason, science,

---

[1]John Boli, Francisco Ramirez, and John Meyer, "Explaining the Origins and Expansion of Mass Education," *Comparative Education Review* 29, no. 2 (1985): 145-170.

and the great books of the Western tradition were sufficient for the task at hand. Certain that they could balance the conflicting demands of classical liberal arts education and schooling for modern, technically based work and professions. The enlightenment project is not dead, just reinvented in both of these influential books.

What is not contained in these discussions is also significant and highlights critical changes in contemporary American intellectual life. For example, no serious doubts are expressed about the possibility of objective knowledge—"facts" are still facts and can be confidently separated from "values." Likewise, no doubts are raised about the possibility of rationally derived, universal ethical principles—there is one way for all Americans to behave, and by teaching students how to think, and by prescribing the right books for them to read, this kind of wise and right behavior will follow. And there are no discussions about intellectual imperialism or the suppression of non-Western cultural and moral traditions, nor discussions of gender, race, ethnicity, or sexual orientation. The kind of cultural diversity debates that enliven our own considerations of general education are not found in these accounts. So, despite what seemed to them to be turbulent times, there is a quaint peacefulness, even a naiveté, to much of the writing. The task of finding academic common ground in postwar America was free of much of our own postmodern contentiousness.

What these distinguished faculties came up with is a vision of general education based squarely on a blend of humanistic and pragmatic principles. The vestiges of the Protestant establishment (Baptist at Chicago and Congregational at Harvard) have been safely confined to extra-curricular life. There are few doubts about the power of human reason to eradicate ignorance and error. We are assured that "however narrow may be the scope of reason's operation, it is within the sphere of these operations that mankind's only hope lies" (Chicago, p. 21), and science is lauded as the best way to "implement the humanism which classicism and Christianity have proclaimed" (Harvard, p. 50). General education requires that "We . . . speak in purely humanistic terms, confining ourselves to the obligation of man to himself and to society" (Harvard, p. 76). It is significant that the Harvard statement about the authority of the "great books" comes in the context of a comparison to the university's earlier reliance on a Protestant reading of Scripture. In this new era, it is classic texts of Greece, Rome, and sixteenth century England that will,

> [open] before students the intellectual forces that have shaped the Western mind. There is a sense in which education in the great books can be looked at as a secular continuation of the spirit of Protestantism. As early Protestantism, rejecting the authority and philosophy of the medieval church, placed reliance on each man's personal reading of Scriptures, so this present movement, rejecting unique authority of the Scripture, places reliance on the reading of those books which are taken to represent the fullest revelation of the Western mind. (Harvard, p. 44)

Combining classical humanism with modern pragmatism did not happen without incident, and it is safe to say that the hearts of these reformers were still with the classic tradition in education. In both books, there is a preoccupation with the problems of "departmentalism" and the rising power of "technique" in the academy. For example, the dean of the College of the University of Chicago cautions that the achievements of academic specialists,

> have been accompanied by a tendency in both teaching and research to mistake the lines which have come to circumscribe the activities of academic departments for divisions in the nature of reality. . . . Something would be wrong . . . with a society in which a lawyer could be a successful lawyer or a merchant could be a successful businessman only by ceasing to be a successful human being. (Chicago, pp. 7-8)

In today's educational climate, and perhaps especially at market-based, tuition-driven institutions, the power of specialized programs and job-oriented departments to attract students, and therefore define the curriculum, is especially strong. As a result, our own conflicts between the liberal arts and professional education resemble those taking place at mid-century in the nation's elite institutions. Now, however, the power of the marketplace to drive educational agendas is even stronger, largely because the political threats posed by fascism and communism have abated, and the nation-building agenda is focused on global economic competition. The driving purpose of higher education at the national, institutional, and personal levels is success in the marketplace, and this utilitarian vision has brought innovation and change to the academy.

At mid-century, the commitment to liberal learning was still pre-eminent. The problem was how to accommodate the economic and technical needs of the nation with the need for free men and women bound together by a common heritage. To build the nation required both liberally educated citizens and specially educated, technically sophisticated workers. The Harvard faculty suggested that,

> a society controlled wholly by specialists is not a wisely ordered society. We cannot, however, turn away from specialism. The problem is how to save general education and its values within a system where specialism is necessary. . . . Thus the two kinds of education once given separately to different social classes must be given together to all alike. (Harvard, p. 53)

Today the debate is generally between traditionalists who ask, "*How* can we save general education and its values?" and those critics who ask "*Why* should we save general education and its values?" Perhaps Christian scholars can provide a third alternative to potentially idolatrous devotion to great books and the Western tradition on the one hand, and postmodern cynicism on the other. From a biblical perspective, what any institution needs is a transcendent critique, not blind subservience or cynical dismissal. Discovering this third way is the task for Christians in academe.

Christians are probably better at stating what we want to do—how our vision of Christian liberal arts would look—than we are of putting this vision into practice. The spirits of our age—scientism, technique, economic growth, for example—subvert our best intentions. We want to challenge students to examine their deepest worldview assumptions about God, human nature, our history and heritage, but it is often more expedient to teach them to do science, to love Shakespeare, to find employment, and to show them how to accommodate their lives to a secular culture. If our commitment to a comprehensive biblical view were really at the center of our enterprise, the result of our work—our own lives as scholars and teachers, the lives of our students, and the life of the university as a whole—would be less like our secular counterparts. What would the university look like if scholarship were transforming rather than conforming?

Christians can learn something from these interesting books. They do give an account of significant events in educational history, and they do describe the origins of many difficulties facing higher education today. Most importantly, they offer real life glimpses of the basic assumptions that have guided educational reform in America. The spirit of humanistic education is articulated with passion and eloquence in these documents. The books bear the imprints of Harvard and the University of Chicago.

The faculty authors were among the most privileged and influential in the world, and they were working to preserve the highest ideals of Western democracy. Underlying the whole edifice is a faith in enlightened values. The God of creation is not a participant in this reforming project; He has, in effect, been required to move off campus, to stay out of the classroom, and find refuge in churches and homes and the private lives of those who still believe. Following the spirit of the Enlightenment, the authors ask much of education, of the Western tradition, of human ingenuity, and of human reason. They wanted to believe in progress, even in the immediate wake of global war and systematic genocide. But there is no transcendent vision here, no "universe of truth sustained by God."[2] We are reminded that educational reform movements are products of the fundamental assumptions and desires of those who create them.

---

[2]George Marsden, *The Outrageous Idea of Christian Scholarship* (New York, NY: Oxford University Press, 1997), 31.

The Seven Liberal Arts in the Middle Ages

edited by David L. Wagner

Reviewed by Dennis O. Royse

The historical development of the seven liberal arts and their place in the fabric of medieval culture are the subjects of *The Seven Liberal Arts in the Middle Ages*, edited by David Wagner. The seven liberal arts include the verbal arts—grammar, rhetoric, dialectic—and the mathematical arts—arithmetic, music, geometry, and astronomy. Wagner's book is based on a lecture series presented at Northern Illinois University during the 1977-78 academic year. In his introductory essay, Wagner traces the development of the liberal arts in the micro-context of prevailing cultural traditions and the macro-context of intellectual history from the Hellenic Age through the High Middle Ages.

Following Wagner's introductory essay is "Incentives for Studying the Liberal Arts" by Karl Morrison. Morrison addresses the question of why the liberal arts were studied. He proposes that by the twelfth century,

---

DENNIS O. ROYSE is an associate professor of music in the School of Music at Azusa Pacific University. He is a graduate of Pasadena College (B.A.), California State University, Los Angeles (M.A.), and Claremont Graduate School (Ph.D.).

liberal arts education was pursued not only for position, wealth, and fame, but also as a means for many scholars to resolve the emotional and intellectual tension between Christianity and classical culture. He states that the adaptation of liberal arts education to the service of Christian doctrine "foretold freedom in a world where one would know without error, rejoice without sorrow, and love without fear" (p. 54).

Each of the seven liberal arts is considered in a subsequent essay by a specialist in the field. Each essay presents a brief description of the conceptual development of the art from the eighth through the tenth centuries and the medieval concept of the art as expressed in the post-classical writings of the Latin encyclopedists. Its cultural impact during the High Middle Ages and twelfth-century Renaissance, and the recovery of ancient Greek learning as preserved in the Moslem world are also discussed.

In the final essay, "Beyond the Liberal Arts," Ralph McInerny discusses the rise of scholasticism and its impact on the liberal arts. He suggests that in the High Middle Ages, liberal arts, scholastic philosophy, and theology were not separate conceptual regions, as many scholars contend, but were components of a greater single vision of knowledge.

Wagner and the other contributing authors relate the following themes regarding the seven liberal arts: (1) As codified by the Latin encyclopedists of the fifth and sixth centuries A.D., they served as the model for Christian culture and education from its beginnings through the twelfth-century Renaissance; (2) Each of the liberal arts was considered a *techne*, a systematic and complete body of knowledge deriving from a clear beginning point or principle. This notion of *techne* reflects their roots in the axiomatic-deductive system of Greek rationalism, primarily Aristotle and Plato; (3) There was never a time when the liberal arts were studied for their own sake but instead they have always been regarded as a *way* to something else. In the early Middle Ages, that something else was the wisdom found in Scripture; and (4) This role of the liberal arts as *ancilla theologiae* was maintained after its realignment to Aristotelian philosophy in the early thirteenth century university, primarily through Thomas Aquinas.

Quoting Raymond Klibansky, Wagner surmises that the seven liberal arts were not just the canon of medieval education and culture but served to "give man both knowledge of the divine and power to express it [and] in so doing, they fulfilled at the same time another purpose. They served *ad cultum hamanitatis*; that is, they promoted the specifically human values, revealing to man his place in the universe and teaching him to appreciate the beauty of the created world."[1]

In his essay on music, Theodore Karp observes that of the seven liberal arts, perhaps none has changed in connotation from antiquity to the present day as much as music. Although its immediate appeal has always been to the senses, it was the ethical power of certain kinds of music to strengthen or weaken character that prompted Plato to treat music so seriously when considering a proper education for his ideal state. Although performers of music in antiquity were well paid, the highest social status was reserved for those who sought after the essence of music (i.e., its measurable aspects). By late antiquity, the *techne* of music was considered a harmonic science of measurable proportions equivalent to that of astronomy. Since music was considered one of the mathematical sciences of the quadrivium, medieval philosophers developed an aesthetic of music based on proportion and number, taking as their beginning point a biblical passage from the *Wisdom of Solomon*, "Thou hast ordered all things in measure and number and weight." Philosophers from St. Augustine to St. Aquinas concluded "that a knowledge of proportion and number was essential to an understanding of God's universe and of the arts, and they incorporated such views into their theological and cosmological constructions" (p. 175).

As an exemplary art, music held a unique place within the quadrivium. By means of analogies, it alone "could help demonstrate connecting links between things sensed, reason and speculation, and ultimately the divine" (p. 175). It is within this analogical construct that Boethius in the sixth century explained his tripartite musical universe. Accordingly, *musica mundana* (the harmony of the world) was concerned with such things as the movements of the heavenly bodies, their proportional relationships, and the changing seasons. It was believed that the orbiting planets produced actual sounds. *Musica humana* (the harmony of the body and soul) was concerned with such things as bodily proportions, humors, the proportions of various virtues and strengths, and the binding together of body and soul. The latter was exemplified in the simultaneous sounding of two

---

[1]Raymond Klibansky, "The School of Chartres," in Marshall Clagett, Gaines Post, and Robert Reynolds, eds., *Twelfth-Century Europe and the Foundations of Modern Society* (Madison, WI: University of Wisconsin Press, 1966), 9-10.

harmonic intervals, i.e., musical harmony. *Musica instrumentalis* was concerned with the nature of sounding music, both instrumental and vocal. Although this Boethian view of music was taught for centuries, the growing need for church music demanded a more practical and pedagogical approach.

One of the first writers to depart from the Boethian view was Guido d' Arezzo (ca. 990-1050), a Benedictine monk responsible for teaching chant to the monastic community. He considered the Boethian view useful to philosophers, but not to singers. Therefore, he included pedagogical devices for teaching the memorization of chant. One of his methods which survives today is the assigning of syllables to specific pitches. For example, the notes *d*, *e*, *f*, *g*, *a*, were assigned the syllables *re*, *mi*, *fa*, *sol*, *la*.

Although the major musical interest of the Middle Ages was concerned with the creation, organization, and preservation of music for the Church, its place as a mathematical discipline in the quadrivium remained compatible with the Christian emphasis on divine order. For some philosophers, music's compatibility to both Christian and classical culture helped to resolve the tension between the two. When the university replaced the cathedral school as the center of learning in the twelfth century, music maintained its exemplary role in the quadrivial arts, lending its unique ability to bring understanding to complex notions. For example, if the term *university* stands for *unity through diversity*, then music is a metaphor of this complex notion, i.e., independent melodic lines creating harmony through diverse motion. According to Karp, it was not until the mid-fifteenth century that mathematics' hold on musical structures gave way considerably in the face of the newer sensual appeals of the Renaissance.

While music was the exemplary art of the quadrivium, grammar held a central position in the arts of the trivium. In his essay on grammar, Jeffrey Huntsman points out that the trivium—grammar, dialectic, and rhetoric—was "concerned with the ordering of experience and the means of giving expression to this knowledge" (p. 60). Accordingly, *dialectic* established a regular and coherent frame for thinking. *Rhetoric* presented models and methods of expression and ultimately of persuasion. "But the foundation discipline, the first road to all knowledge, was *grammar*" (p. 60). Grammar was thought to discipline the mind and the soul at the same time, honing the intellectual and spiritual abilities that the future cleric would need to read and speak with discernment.

As a *techne*, the organizing principle of grammar was the *word*. As its first major topic, the *word* began with a discussion of individual letters. "The examination of words turned next to syllables, and generally also included pronunciation and orthography, etymology, and analogy. The eight parts of speech were a second major topic, with analyses of the vices and virtues of speech the third and final topic" (p. 58).

As the underlying system of medieval grammar was founded on the same assumptions as most other medieval disciplines of inquiry and explanation, it is not surprising to find developmental similarities between them. Just as practical and philosophical beliefs developed regarding the art of music, the same general beliefs were expressed regarding the art of grammar. According to Huntsman, one set of beliefs addressed the practical needs of the teacher concerned with instilling in students a Latin that was at once grammatically proper and rhetorically effective. This was regarded as necessary for several reasons: to function in the world of commerce and trade, to understand science and philosophy, and above all, to read and understand Scripture. This practical pedagogical approach focused primarily on Donatus' teaching texts and Priscian's work which used the Latin classics as examples of literary and grammatical excellence. It was not until the late twelfth century that new types of pedagogical grammars began to appear.

In contrast to these practical grammars, another branch of medieval linguistics addressed the scholar's more abstract concern with understanding the nature of language itself. Just as the Boethian view of music attempted to exemplify the world musico-mathematically, these philosophical grammars attempted to explain the world using the organizational principles found in languages. Likewise, as the speculative writers on music considered the manners or *modes* of music (a mode is a scale), the studies of the speculative grammarians centered on the several manners or modes of language and thought (hence their name Modistae grammarians). It is interesting to note that the word *modus* in this context meant *way*, implying that the study of grammar leads to an understanding of something greater than itself. According to Huntsman, the Modistae were teachers of grammar, not of Latin. Their subject was the language of thinking: "thus the initiating impulse, the efficient cause, was what gave language its most interesting features." He concludes that "in our time we have witnessed a reawakening to the aesthetic values of medieval art, music, and architecture. It is time we recognized as well the achievements of the medieval intellectuals whose object of study was our language and mind" (p. 85).

In considering the relevance of the themes presented above to Christian higher education, one is drawn to a recurring theme and an underlying tension. The recurring theme, indeed the underlying tenet, is that the liberal arts have historically been regarded as a means to an end beyond themselves. While Christian culture has always claimed the liberal arts as the road to enlightenment (i.e., knowledge of God and creation as found in Scripture), secular culture has considered them a means to a different end (i.e., knowledge for the sake of knowledge). This tension is the backdrop against which the liberal arts tradition has developed, attempting to reconcile harmony and discord while ministering to many masters.

Today, Christian higher education continues the synthesizing efforts of William of Conches, Hugh of St. Victor, and Thomas Aquinas, choosing to view the liberal arts as part of a greater vision of knowledge and finding continuity and overlap as well as distinctions between the various disciplines of the mind. "The arts are part of a larger whole, a whole that, as Thomas Aquinas sees it, is capped by theology, and we may . . . grow old in the study of ultimate causes. Does wisdom entail a repudiation of the arts? Surely it is the mark of the wise man that he remains true to the dreams of his youth" (p. 267). The dream of the liberal arts tradition is as relevant to Christian higher education today as it was to the ancients: to bring us to knowledge of the Creator, of creation, and of our relationship to both.

A Quest for Common Learning
by Ernest L. Boyer and Arthur Levine

Reviewed by Cahleen M. Shrier

Commissioned by the Carnegie Foundation for the Advancement of Teaching, Ernest Boyer and Arthur Levine address issues surrounding general education in *A Quest For Common Learning*. They surveyed college catalogs at three hundred and nine American higher education institutions, examining the purpose, content, and process of general education at these institutions. Fifty *different* purposes were identified, leading them to conclude that there is no common understanding of what general education is or what it should look like (p. 24). The authors find this variety confusing, and, in response, they provide a working definition for readers. General education, they say, is "the learning that should be common to all people" (p. viii).

The common learning of all people, according to Boyer and Levine, cannot be accomplished through many traditional strategies. For example, general education requirements cannot be met by simply picking courses from organized lists, as in the "smorgasbord distribution approach." They give the example of an English requirement being met by either a

---

CAHLEEN M. SHRIER is an assistant professor of biology in the College of Liberal Arts and Sciences at Azusa Pacific University. She is a graduate of Southern California College (B.A.), and Loma Linda University (M.S., Ph.D.).

"course on literature from creation to the Renaissance; a course on Faulkner; or even courses on journalism, film, or creative writing." They are adamant that "this is not general education!" (p. 30). Required core courses do not necessarily provide general education either. Rather, from their perspective, general education is the deliberate presentation of common course content. The presentation of this common content may come in a variety of ways, however, while still achieving the same purpose (p. 47).

The book also makes a distinction between general education and liberal education. While general education refers to the study of common course content, liberal education refers to the whole range of experiences encountered by a student while pursuing an education. Involvement in music, drama, athletics, forensics, community service, campus clubs, residence life, general education requirements, the academic major, and electives all play a role in liberal education. General education is merely a segment of the overall liberal education experience. The goals of general education need to be distinguished from the aims of liberal education so that its contribution remains proportional to the total experience (p. 32).

The authors also provide a historical picture of the general education movements in America. They argue that developments in general education can be organized as three "revivals." Although general education is continually subject to reforms, there appear to be periods when the rate of reform accelerates as a result of increased emphasis on the campuses (p. 9). These time periods include 1918-30, 1943-55, and 1971-81. Boyer and Levine conclude that each of these revivals was catalyzed by societal events such as World War I and World War II, and that they were not a result of on-campus issues. Immediately following these wars, societal bonds were weak and the idea of the individual gained strength. It was hoped that general education would cure the fragmentation which was occurring in society and was mirrored in the academic arena. The role of general education was to combat "vocationalism, overspecialization and elective curriculum" (p. 15). "[W]e suggest that it is precisely at these times, when social bonds are weakened, that general education movements take root" (p. 18).

After discussing the history of general education and its definitions, Boyer and Levine state that the purpose of general education is to develop an understanding of ourselves as connected to the world as a whole, an idea much like the one that sparked earlier revivals. This can be accomplished by coming to the "recognition that beyond our individual differences lie fundamental human relationships, common experiences, and collective concerns that can and must be thoughtfully explored by all students" (p. 31). To realize this goal requires a curriculum through which,

> all students examine the distinctions we make between beliefs and "facts," and how values are formed, transmitted, and revised. They should examine, too, the values currently held in our society, looking at the ways such values are socially enforced, and how societies react to unpopular beliefs. General education should introduce all students to the powerful role political ideologies, and particularly religion, have played in shaping, throughout history, the convictions of individuals and societies. (p. 44)

Boyer and Levine alleviate potential fears that general education would create intellectual clones by claiming its goals are not to,

> promote intellectual conformity or a sterile acquiescence to the notion of social cohesion. . . . The kind of general education we envisage will focus on issues about which people feel most deeply, on points where conflict and controversy are most likely to occur. What will be shared is not a common set of conclusions, but a common agenda for study and investigation and a common discourse. (p. 19)

They continue to console the anxious reader by defining "agenda" as "those experiences, relationships, and ethical concerns that are common to all of us simply by virtue of our membership in the human family at a particular moment in history." Boyer and Levine believe that responding to individual interests and vocational needs is necessary but not sufficient in the educational process. They remind readers that this idea has been around for a long time in various forms, and that they are not proposing anything new (p. 19).

While these authors do not address Christian higher education per se, their stated purpose for general education is clearly compatible with a Christian worldview. In the New Testament, Jesus collapses the ten commandments into two: (1) "Love the Lord your God with all your heart, and with all your soul, and with all your mind, and with all your strength"; and (2) "Love your neighbor as yourself" (Mark 12:30-31). These two commandments provide the governing principles for Christian education. Christian institutions need to both impart knowledge *and* direct students to love God and love their neighbor. Otherwise we are indistinct from secular institutions. If general education leads to a greater awareness of the student as an individual and also as one connected to the larger world, it may lay the foundation for understanding one's neighbor and lead toward a loving spirit. This would be consistent with Christian higher education. While it is possible to have faith that this could occur, it is still necessary to support such a claim with the appropriate evidence.

The authors are to be commended for defining the problem of general education, and for going a step further and proposing a solution. They have devised a curriculum that they believe will achieve the goals of general education and that will guide students to "understand that they share with others the use of symbols, membership in groups and institutions, the activities of production and consumption, a relationship with nature, a sense of time, and commonly held values and beliefs" (p. 35). Under each of these six general education themes, the authors produce a lengthy list of concepts they propose as a foundation for common learning (pp. 36-45).

The emphasis is on presenting all students with these six themes; however, the method of teaching this common content does not appear to be important. It may take the form of core courses, survey courses, seminars, special speakers, film clips, theme courses, interdisciplinary courses, et cetera. (pp. 46-47). The content must be evaluated on "whether students are helped to understand the shared relationships common to all people" (p. 46). They conclude that "it seems quite clear to us that an exploration of these connections is indispensable if students are adequately to understand themselves, their society, and the world in which they live" (p. 35). How Boyer and Levine came to this conclusion is unclear.

Boyer and Levine call for a *fourth* revival of general education that will emphasize our interdependence within the larger world. This is necessary because "today's students are the products of a society in which the call for individual gratification booms forth on every side while the social claim is weak and enfeebled" (p. 19). The students described in *A Quest for Common Learning* were enrolled in the late 1970s to early 1980s. Their fierce individualism weakly connects them to the larger society (p. 19). They are also portrayed by the authors as more cynical than the prior generation, and as having pessimistic attitudes toward the future of the nation and the world. However, students were hopeful concerning their own future and, therefore, they turned inward in their attempts to succeed (p. 20). Some parallels seem to exist between the group of students depicted in the book and Generation X.[1]

The authors suggest a remedy for this unconnected society. They state that to reconnect ourselves to society it is essential for us to understand ourselves to be interdependent within the larger world. They cite as an example Colin Turnbull's study of a North African tribe that once flourished, but has since "crumbled." The tribe's disintegration was attributed to the loss of its "social cement," consisting of the tribe's "heritage, values, and mutual relationships." The authors prophetically proclaim that this collapse could occur within our society. To guard against such a possibility, general education has an "urgent role" to emphasize "those experiences that knit isolated individuals into a community" (p. 35). Boyer and Levine suggest that general education provides the "social cement" that will prevent our society from crumbling. This seems to be an implicit theme throughout the book.

But is general education capable of preserving a society and preventing it from collapse? It appears that Boyer and Levine join a long list of individuals who view general education as a potent cure for societal ailments (pp. 6-8). Though such an assumption may seem intuitive, the authors do not provide data to support the assumption that general education fosters the recognition of ourselves as connected to the larger world. Neither their extensive survey of the historical literature discussing general education nor their evaluation of academic catalogs has provided evidence that their proposed purpose for general education is actually achieved. No measured outcomes are presented to assess whether or not general education is a successful means to this end.

To conclude, if the applications proposed by Boyer and Levine are valid, they will probably also apply to the student of the twenty-first century. Students today frequently come from single parent families, have little contact with extended family members, and may not even

---

[1]Douglas Coupland describes the members of Generation X as follows: they are cynical; they assume they will divorce; they are not concerned with their family or extended family; they tend to feel that voting is not important; and they have trouble sustaining relationships. While these are broad generalizations, an element of truth appears to exist in Coupland's description. *Generation X* (New York, NY: St. Martin's Press, 1991).

know their ethnic heritage. All these factors contribute to an even greater disconnectedness from the surrounding world. This may support the idea of providing a common education that allows the student to be connected to their neighbor. But can general education really provide the connectedness that this generation is lacking?

The Closing of the American Mind

by Allan Bloom

Reviewed by Gayle Beebe

There is a growing body of literature produced by distinguished thinkers from various disciplines that uncover the loss of a unifying ideal within American thought and culture. They all show the inadequacies of this development and suggest that we have been cut off from the rich cultural resources which provide understanding for ourselves and meaning and direction for our lives. According to these writers, we have arrived at a serious intellectual crisis in Western culture which is making it impossible to sustain any meaningful vision of the nature and destiny of human life.

This literature includes Robert Bellah's *Habits of the Heart* and *The Good Society*; Alasdair MacIntyre's *After Virtue*; Basil Mitchell's *Morality, Religious and Secular*; Charles Taylor's *Sources of the Self*; Leszek Kolakowski's *Modernity on Endless Trial*; and John Milbank's

---

GAYLE BEEBE is professor of pastoral theology and dean of the C. P. Haggard School of Theology at Azusa Pacific University. He is a graduate of George Fox College (B.A.), Princeton Theological Seminary (M.Div.), and Claremont Graduate School (MBA, Ph.D.).

Theology and Social Theory. But of all these works, the most poignant and controversial is Allan Bloom's brilliant contribution, *The Closing of the American Mind*, which highlights this crisis within our colleges and universities.

The heart of Bloom's argument is that the university has lost its original reason for existence. According to Bloom, the university was once the place where society produced great citizens by raising the great questions of life and then providing the atmosphere within which one could both consider and pursue significant answers to these questions. Today, however, this is not the case. Instead, the university has capitulated to the avalanche of moral relativism and now offers a carnival of titillating options with no unifying ideal. As a result, education no longer produces great human beings, but only specialists capable of the application and perfection of particular techniques.

This has forfeited the soul of today's colleges and universities and the students and faculties who inhabit them. If the real motive of education was once the pursuit of the highest aspirations of the human soul, it is now simply the pursuit of professional skills ensuring access to the good life of conspicuous consumption. We have become intellectual prodigals who squander our inheritance on wanton pleasures without finding any meaning or sustaining purpose in our life.

By comparison, the goal of liberal education, according to Bloom, is to break the shackles of our brute existence in order to pursue the highest good. This pursuit, moreover, requires conviction and conviction requires commitment. We must believe that there is more to life than we have encountered so far, and then be committed to finding this life.

Liberal education once cultivated such conviction and demanded such commitment, but Bloom argues that all vision for liberal education has been lost. We are not better educated, as some claim, which once meant to be in touch with higher ideals accessible nowhere else. Now we have a vast wasteland of curricular options with no guidance and no governing purpose other than the fulfillment of the basic requirements needed for a degree.

For Bloom, liberal education, at its best, must strive to find whatever it is in students that yearns for completion and then provide the resources that satisfy this yearning. Unfortunately, this yearning has been seduced and replaced by the complete preoccupation with the here and now. This preoccupation has given rise to unbridled lust for instant gratification. If liberal education once built bridges between our life and the resources that can sustain our life, it has now utterly abandoned such work in pursuit of unbridled hedonism.

Bloom is particularly concerned to answer this question: What do we mean when we say a student is educated? The lack of any guidance in addressing this question reflects the lack of any unifying ideal in the university curriculum. As a result, educators have become more concerned with packaging curriculum than with its content. Schools no longer strive to satisfy our deepest longings for completion; they simply dispense degrees.

The antidote proposed by Bloom is not an attempt to reassert the "great books" curriculum, but to reassert that a precise, synoptic approach like the "great books" curriculum is still needed. Texts that raise life's most significant questions should be chosen, and then approaches to addressing these questions should be offered. Thus, for Bloom, a liberal education at its best should both cultivate and feed a student's need and desire for truth and the good life. This is the key responsibility of the university and the chief argument Bloom raises in pleading for the revitalization of liberal education across the university curriculum.

Before turning to the implications of Bloom's work for Christian liberal arts education, a few caveats are in order. First, although Bloom's book is clearly a landmark in cultural analysis and educational philosophy, he is an unrepentant Europhile. In his quest to show our reliance on all things European, he fails to elevate even one American author who contributed to the shape and fabric of American life. Missing is any significant commentary on Thomas Jefferson, Benjamin Franklin, James Madison, *The Federalist Papers*, Abraham Lincoln, Henry Clay, or even Carl Becker. And literary contributions are lacking as well. The thesis that runs through the entire treatise would find ample support from Walker Percy, John Steinbeck, Stephen Crane, Nathaniel Hawthorne, Herman Melville, Harriet Beecher Stowe, and many others. My point is not to add to the burden of his analysis, but simply to highlight that he shows no conversation with those American sources that would add credence to his ideal.

Second, Bloom uses value-laden terms in confusing ways. For example, best and better have different meanings in different contexts. At some places, best and better mean the most talented students. At others, best and better mean the most moral students. This slight confusion reflects a general tendency throughout Bloom's treatise to imply that the best (i.e., brightest) students are the best (i.e., moral) citizens.

Finally, Bloom misses the uniquely American reality that education in America has always been a blend of liberal arts and career advancement. Of all the robber barons of the late nineteenth-century, for example, only Cornelius Vanderbilt had been to college, and this for only one year. Yet all of the most prominent robber barons gave vast amounts of their fortunes to build the very bastions of liberal inquiry Bloom so prizes. This should serve as a reminder that liberal education in America has always wedded the active and the contemplative in the same curriculum.

Although these concerns need to be noted, they do not detract from Bloom's brilliant critique of education in America. The implications of his work for Christian liberal arts education are profound. The purpose of Christian liberal arts education is to teach us how to order our lives and minds in an effort to connect us to God. Despite contemporary skepticism of metanarratives and transcultural moralities, there is a growing awareness that historically and culturally contingent values can connect us to universal ideals that provide meaning and direction for our lives. Thus, the chief responsibility of Christian liberal arts education is to teach us how to relate every historical and cultural value to the transcendent good that is God.

Our culture has lost confidence in any universal, unifying moral ideal. In fact, as Bloom so effectively documents, the only universal moral ideal within our culture is that there are no universal moral ideals. Yet, culture and communities shape individuals in particular ways.

Thus, what a Christian liberal arts education can provide is the recognition that individuals have particular identities, developed within particular families, shaped by particular cultures and communities, all of which elevate one to universal, all encompassing ideals. In this context, Christian liberal arts education can show that humans are both great and wretched, why we are this way, where our remedy lies, how we can obtain it, and what kind of life we will lead as a result of embracing this remedy. This is a fundamental reorientation from the way education is typically packaged: either as a necessary rite of passage or as an essential step in launching one's career. Instead, Christian liberal arts education helps us identify those values within our culture worth sustaining and helps us reorient those values that need modification in order to express the fullness of a Christian view of life.

Bloom is absolutely correct when he shows how Eros' longing for completion has been distracted by our lower longings for physical pleasures. This disorientation has disordered and corrupted our life. To recover, however, means to reestablish an orienting center for our entire university. The proper center for a Christian university is God and the proper curriculum for a Christian liberal arts university is to order the life and mind of our students so as to incline their hearts and minds to God. The obvious fear in such a proposal is that this affirmation will become another thin veil for indoctrination.

Christian liberal arts education must resist this temptation in order to cultivate within our students a vision for the destiny of their life, both temporally and eternally. It is not the mastery of technique, although it may include such mastery. Instead, Christian liberal arts education must be the cultivation of wisdom and insight and the opportunity to develop such wisdom and insight by exposure to and guidance in the great questions of life.

This is possible at a Christian liberal arts university when we develop the moral and intellectual life properly and so are able to explore every facet of a liberal arts curriculum from the perspective of a Christian. In order to create this opportunity, we must explore the great questions of life from the conviction that God exists and that every aspect of human knowledge can be an opportunity to understand God more fully.

Within the tradition of Christianity, there exists great confidence in the human intellect. But like Bloom, Christian thinkers from Augustine and Aquinas to Evagrius and Maximus have argued that the intellectual life can be compromised by unbridled pursuit of physical desires. When pursued properly, however, the intellectual life provides us with access to another world, a world of sustainable values and eternal ideals. It is in this domain that one finally encounters a unifying ideal that can provide coherence and meaning for our temporal life as we move towards fulfilling our eternal destiny.

The Meaning of General Education

by Gary E. Miller

Reviewed by Roger White

In light of changing societal goals and cultural influences, Gary Miller seeks to clarify an emerging definition for the general education curriculum in higher education. The focus of the work is not the content of this curriculum but rather the conceptual and theoretical base which informs practice. In the process of characterizing the change in views toward general education, liberal education is also considered.

According to Miller, general education began in the 1920s and 1930s as a reform movement addressing the overly specialized emphasis of the liberal arts approach in higher education. Highly influenced by naturalistic humanism and instrumentalism, its goal was to produce a more functionally utilitarian student. The general education curriculum focused on the needs and interests of students and the relationship between the individual and contemporary democratic society. Concentrating on the lifelong learning

---

ROGER WHITE is an associate professor of education in the School of Education and Behavioral Studies at Azusa Pacific University. He is a graduate of East Tennessee State University (B.S.), Reformed Theological Seminary (M.C.E., M.Ed.), and University of Tennessee (Ed.D.).

process and the experiential, general education emphasizes the present and future rather than the past. Its primary aim is preparing individuals to solve contemporary and future social problems. Curricular attention is given primarily to method rather than content.

Following this preliminary definition of general education, Miller addresses some of the influences that have shaped and challenged this understanding. His observations on three of these influences are summarized here:

1. ***New conceptions of democracy affect the goal of general education.*** As the nation's view of democracy has changed over the years, the practice of general education has been affected. Where democracy had once been seen as a *process*, after World War II it became viewed more as an *institution*. This tended to confuse the direction of general education curriculum since the means of its educational methodology (emphasis on process) no longer matched its educational ends. When the public's view of American democracy shifted, so did its embrace of general education.

2. ***The increase of interdisciplinary offerings in the higher education curriculum tend to confuse the scope of general education.*** Interdisciplinary study is not synonymous with general education, but was originally a response to a fragmented curriculum and sought to provide a breadth of understanding across the disciplines. Too often, though, interdisciplinary study becomes an end in itself with a highly specialized authority structure and delimited educational goals putting it at odds with the aims of general education. General education may incorporate an interdisciplinary approach, but this is done with a view to its own instrumentalist ends.

3. ***The demands of vocationalism have caused a reconceptualizing of the nature of general education.*** Narrow vocational training which provides only a single trade's narrow skill base is incongruous with the process emphasis of general education. On the other hand, the increasing growth and development of technology demands a strong curricular presence in the general education program in order to help students relate to and deal with the complexities and difficulties of new advancements.

While these and other trends broaden popular conceptions of general education, Miller insists that the growing number of adult learners, as well as continuing education programs that tend to demand immediate applicability and usefulness of academic studies, continue to find the pragmatic approach of general education useful and attractive. General education remains concerned with the individual student and that student's relationship to community. It is not simply the first two years of undergraduate instruction, nor is it merely a carefully prescribed curriculum. The goal of general education has always focused on the need of the individual and democratically informed and delivered instruction.

In contrast to this treatment of general education, the author also briefly considers liberal education. The following distinctions are made:

> Liberal education, founded on rationalist assumptions, oriented toward essentialism, and based in the methods of logic, is concerned with ideas in the abstract, with the conservation of universal truths handed down through the years and with the development of the intellect. General education, founded on instrumentalist assumptions, oriented toward existentialism, and based on psychological methods, is concerned with experimentation and problem solving for individual and social action, with the problems of the present and future, and with the development of the individual. (p. 183)

It is important for the reader to recognize that the two approaches to education have different starting and ending points. Therein is our concern for Christian higher education. Many schools uncritically adopt educational philosophies and practices without considering the associated foundational assumptions and prescribed ends, nor do they consider how they ultimately relate to historic Christian faith positions. The resulting curriculum often perpetuates the thrust of the errant philosophies. Unfortunately, some educators believe that if they baptize general education and liberal education with a vague Christian ethos and then combine it with a generic love ethic expressed primarily through "modeling," the result will be "Christian education." However, the Christian worldview has starting and ending points that must supersede and qualify the goals and purposes of general or liberal education.

Liberal education's view of "universal truth" must be interpreted in light of historic Christianity's revelatory truth claims. General education's short-term pragmatic benefits must be contextualized into ultimate life purposes considered from the eternal perspectives present in a Christian worldview. Short-sighted educators may believe they are serving students by helping them "gain knowledge" and providing them "critical thinking skills," but we are remiss when we ignore and exclude from instruction the core purposes of being in a right relationship to the Creator and of being responsible image-bearers, messengers, and stewards of His creation.

A further confusion results in Christian colleges when the short-term goals of general education and the knowledge transmission of liberal education are seen simply in terms of service to the community at large. The primary responsibility of preparing Christians and equipping the saints becomes a nondirectional, undefined "doing good to all people," which of course hardly distinguishes the Christian enterprise from its secular counterparts. The distinctively Christian message is absent. At too many Christian institutions, evangelical students arrive on campus and absorb a vague, detached, "do good" message. They are on their own in trying to figure out how their education relates to ultimate faith issues. The conscientious Christian student ends up sitting alone in the classroom.

In this postmodern era, educators at Christian colleges and universities must recognize that it is impossible to deliver education in a perspective-free vacuum. An interpretive framework is required and wholesale adoption of general education or liberal education approaches carry with them inherent assumptions about humanity and reality that are often incongruent with the Christian faith.

New Life for the College Curriculum

by Jerry G. Gaff

Reviewed by Maximo Rossi

More than any other academic domain, liberal education has been the target of attacks and criticisms from every conceivable quarter. Allan Bloom, for instance, has accused academia of masterminding the closing of young minds and allegedly impoverishing their intellect through "American simplicity." Ronald Nash, on the other hand, claims that the root of the problem is the superficial relativism of an educational system that closes the very heart of the young.[1] In *New Life for the College Curriculum*, Jerry Gaff explains the matter in simpler terms: "College-bashing . . . has become a national pastime" (p. xi). The fact is American liberal education has been at the core of heated debate and dynamic reform for the last two decades, and *New Life for the College Curriculum* attempts to assess the result of this struggle.

MAXIMO ROSSI is an associate professor of modern languages, chair of the Department of Modern Languages, and associate dean of the College of Liberal Arts and Sciences at Azusa Pacific University. He is a graduate of The King's College (B.A.), Syracuse University (M.A.), and City University of New York (Ph.D.).

[1]Allan Bloom, *The Closing of the American Mind* (New York, NY: Simon and Schuster, 1987). Ronald Nash, *The Closing of the American Heart* (Dallas, TX: Probe Books, 1990).

Gaff deals primarily with the historical and present reforms of the college curriculum. The argument over curriculum reform is divided into three main parts: (1) the debate over the reform of the curriculum; (2) the assessment of the impact of these reforms; and (3) the support of these improvements to the curriculum. Consequently, the first part of the book summarizes the major reform accomplishments to date and examines the public debate about quality education. Among these attainments are the rediscovery by educators of the liberal arts and sciences in the aftermath of the vocational education tendency of the 1970s and 1980s; the emphasis on fundamental skills such as writing, foreign languages, and mathematics; and the tightening of curricular structure as well as higher standards and more rigorous requirements. The second part of the book is an assessment of the changes outlined in the first part, with special attention to the positive impact of comprehensive curricular changes to colleges and universities. Part three points to organizational support for maintaining and upholding changes that are made in the curriculum.

Gaff concludes the book with a call for a future agenda to keep the spirit of reform alive with a campuswide commitment to providing students with a broad general education. The book, then, studies general education reform from an institutional perspective since it centers on actual college curricula, rather than offering an individual, theoretical perspective of what the college curriculum ought to be.

In addition, Gaff argues that the debate over liberal education can be divided into four main areas or what he calls the four Cs: content, coherence, commonality, and comprehensiveness. Although critics agree concerning the need for high-quality education, all too few agree on how this should be done. The first C deals with the questions of what the students should *know* (knowledge), what they should *be able to do* (skills), and what kind of people they should *become* (personal qualities). The answers to these questions provide the platform for a definition of liberal education: academic training charged with bringing knowledge and skills together and integrating them in order to form a wholly functional human being.

The second C declares that, along with rigorous content, the college curriculum should also be coherent. According to Gaff, fragmentation characterizes most curricula, especially in general education. Regretfully, higher education dismantled the curriculum structure in the 1960s and 1970s by allowing students to pick and choose their own courses.

The third C asserts that commonality should be exalted above individuality. General education should concern itself with providing learning experiences that remind students of their common kinship with the human family. To support this point Gaff quotes Boyer and Levine who state that general education ***is*** "common learning" (p. 23).

The fourth C states that "a comprehensive rethinking is necessary to determine what students should learn, how they should be taught, and what organizational and administrative support is needed" (p. 25). Liberal education differs from other educational methods in that liberal education does not emphasize specialization in any one area of study, but rather draws from many fields as a means of forming broadly trained human beings.

There is significant correlation between Gaff's objective of forming broadly trained human beings with a deep sense of shared humanity and the objectives of Christian higher education. In the words of Arthur Holmes, liberal education,

> has to do with the making of persons, Christian education with the making of Christian persons. Since this is what God's creative and redemptive work is about—the making of persons in His own image—it follows that an education that helps make us more fully persons is especially important to Christians.[2]

The author's thesis, then, affirms that all changes in the liberal studies curriculum that lead to better structures for supporting undergraduate general education are necessary and must be upheld and applauded. The greatest strengths of Gaff's arguments are the thoroughness of his sources: he surveyed three hundred colleges and universities involved in general education reform; he enlisted the participation of chief academic officers, who completed lengthy questionnaires and submitted material about their general education programs; and, finally, he called upon his personal experiences as director of the Project on General Education Models

---

[2] Arthur Holmes, *The Idea of a Christian College*, revised edition (Grand Rapids, MI: Eerdmans, 1987), 25.

(GEM), and his service as dean of the college, acting college president, and vice president for planning. These sources and experiences lend his arguments and claims an aura of thoroughness and credibility.

Two perceived weaknesses may be that he is now writing from *outside* of academia having taken "leave from campus demands" (p. xiii). In addition, his discussion lacks a prescriptive or normative stance for a clearer definition of the nature of liberal education.

Prescribing the Life of the Mind

by Charles Anderson

Reviewed by Roxane Lulofs

Higher education, Charles Anderson points out, is one of the most expensive purchases Americans make, second only to a home. In our consumer-based society, education's high price means that it is a valued good. Moreover, American education is generally seen as superior to that found in other countries. It stands to reason, then, that educators would want to make this expensive endeavor clearly worth the price that is paid, critiquing it as needed and constantly questioning whether its practices are good. Working against the task of critiquing the university, Anderson argues, is the fact that we have come to see its ways as natural. It is hard to imagine an alternative.

Given Anderson's title—*Prescribing the Life of the Mind: An Essay on the Purpose of the University, the Aims of Liberal Education, the Competence of Citizens, and the Cultivation of Practical Reason*—one might well expect a complete re-visioning of the university and its

---

ROXANE LULOFS is professor of communication in the College of Liberal Arts and Sciences at Azusa Pacific University. She is a graduate of University of Southern California (B.A.), Azusa Pacific University (B.A.), Purdue University (M.S.), and University of Southern California (Ph.D.).

purposes. Such a vision would include not only goals for universities but would also provide methods for implementing the new vision. While Anderson begins the task of re-visioning and prescription, he does not really carry it through to completion.

Anderson starts with a basic question concerning the purpose of a university: While the author claims that "education is the public purpose of the university and inquiry its basic function," he also points out that he does not think that "we expect the university to teach just as the citizens want or just as the academics deem fit" (pp. 42–43). Thus, the central question of higher education is this: What can we do to better prepare people to think, plan, judge, empathize, wonder, hypothesize, criticize, test, invent, and imagine?

Anderson considers several models of education that he rejects as inadequate. The model of enculturation fails because it depends on customs and traditions that may no longer be of value for our society. The model of educating citizens fails because the doctrine of education may be changed depending upon the whims of people informing the doctrine. The model of utility, preparing people for professions, is not sufficient, particularly in light of the fact that so many people change professions in their lifetimes. And the model of character building is inadequate because there is no one to arbitrate the particular character traits that should be cultivated. (The alert reader might argue with Anderson that preparing people to think, plan, judge, and so forth is the inculcation of character traits.) Anderson makes the argument that only through the cultivation of practical reason can the university serve the purpose to which it has been called. Practical reason is "concerned specifically with how things ought to be done, with good and bad performance, correctness and error, and all of this in relation to some clear conception of point and purpose" (p. 36).

To that end, Anderson proposes five "sequences of thought" that could be taught in universities. The first level would be *mastery*, where students endeavor to learn how to do something as well as it can be done. The second level would be *critical reason*, where students would learn to criticize and correct their own performances, then learn to criticize the performances of others, then learn to criticize the practice itself. The third level would be the *art of judgment*, where students would learn that it is possible to think otherwise about the matter at hand. At the fourth level would be *creativity* and *innovation*, where students learn to come up with new approaches to problem solving. The last sequence of thought would be *transcendence*, where students learn to answer questions concerning the meaning of what they are doing. Anderson asserts,

> I have said that the purpose of the university, through all the ages, was to find out what could be done with the powers of the mind. I have also said that the heart of any system of practical reason is the examination of present practice, to see if we can do better. Thus, in a program of liberal education founded on the cultivation of these habits of mind, ultimate questions *will* arise, routinely, automatically, as a matter of course. For simply to be clear about our purposes, and thus to appraise our performance, to ask whether we have taught people to think well or poorly, *we will eventually have to ask what the mind is supposed to be doing in the world.* (p. 117)

In his effort to define what the mind should be doing, Anderson proposes a new university curriculum that would be organized around several broad areas. Some of these areas are content-based—students would learn about civilization, science, the human situation, and the humanities. In other areas of study, such as practical philosophy, students would learn new habits of the mind. Finally, practical studies would contain the best that each discipline has to offer in terms of practical knowledge. These practical studies might include writing and speaking skills, computation skills, and so on. Anderson offers this new and improved curriculum in opposition to the traditional (and limited) notion of liberal education, where students select among a menu of options. He argues,

> The function of the [traditional] liberal education courses, the "breadth" requirements, is simply to introduce students to the diverse professional disciplines. Most instructors unquestioningly assume that the function of the basic courses, the "core" liberal arts curriculum, is to "interest" students in their subject and provide instruction necessary for more advanced work; in other words, to recruit and prepare potential majors. . . . Are we to understand then that the aim of liberal education is to provide a kind of "exhibit" of the works of the university? Is it our intent that the liberally educated person is one who is well acquainted with the academic division of labor? (p. 34)

While Anderson suggests a curriculum, and while he asserts that the traditional antipathy between science and religion is largely artificial and ought to be ignored, he provides no real instruction as to how a Christian university might accomplish the aims that he has suggested, saying only that "Perhaps there should be a political, a religious, or an economic *dimension* to the university's teaching. But I do not think we would be willing to define any one of these objectives as the essential point of the university" (p. 40).

I beg to differ. I am quite willing to define a religious *dimension*, indeed, a religious *mission*, as the essential point of some universities. No university that defines itself as "Christian" can fail to identify thoughtful and systematic integration of faith and learning as its central objective. Further, I cannot fathom how one might accomplish the teaching of practical reason without values based on political, religious, or economic dimensions. There is no value-free learning. No university can accomplish the teaching of practical reason (i.e., teaching people how to think) without a value-based approach. All theories of science and humanity rely on implicit beliefs, beliefs about who God is, and beliefs about who people are in relationship to God. If we do not explicitly define the values upon which the learning at our institutions will be based, those values will emerge through haphazard and uneven teaching and application, particularly when "the average academic department has no more people of genuine intellectual zest and broad enthusiasm than one is apt to find at a convention of stockmen, charter fishing boat operators, city managers, or restaurateurs" (p. 26). Ultimately, Anderson's essay makes large assertions but leaves us approximately where we started.

Orators and Philosophers

by Bruce Kimball

and

The Condition of American Liberal Education

edited by Robert Orrill

Reviewed by James Hedges

According to Bruce Kimball, you are probably biased in favor of either the oratorical or the philosophical tradition in the liberal arts. To find out, try this simple test:

T F 1. Liberal education and liberal arts have become synonymous.

T F 2. Liberal education is based on reading and understanding key "classic" texts.

T F 3. Liberal education is based on the disinterested pursuit of truth.

JAMES HEDGES is professor of English and chair of the Department of English at Azusa Pacific University. He is a graduate of Seattle Pacific University (B.A.), University of Washington (M.A.), and University of California, Riverside (Ph.D.).

T F 4. Liberal education derives from Socrates.
T F 5. Liberal education derives from Cicero.
T F 6. Liberal education focuses on developing character and values.
T F 7. Liberal education focuses on preparation for specialized education (majors, research).
T F 8. Liberal education relates to "freeing" or liberating the individual.
T F 9. Liberal education relates to "leisure" and is for an elite class.
T F 10. "Liberal arts education" is just a term to justify general education requirements.

If you answered True to 2, 5, and 9, you are biased toward the oratorical tradition of liberal arts. If you answered True to 3, 4, 7, and 8, you are biased toward the philosophic tradition. Both traditions hold to 1 and 6. If you answered True to 10, you are a cynic.

Of course it is not that simple. But Kimball's study of liberal education from its origins in classical antiquity does identify two distinctive ideals, still embedded in the current controversy over the nature and content of the liberal arts. With painstaking particularity, Kimball traces the two ideals, showing how one or the other has dominated at different times, and why. This enables us to recognize the background behind opposing arguments over what liberal education is and ought to be. And as with all history, we may thus see more clearly the implications of the choices we make in configuring liberal education within a Christian worldview as well.

The older of the two traditions may be called oratorical. Proposed by Cicero, it derived from Isocrates' quarrel with the philosophers about the supremacy of oratory over philosophy because it requires one to be able both to express the philosophy held and to persuade others to virtue. Following Quintilian's lead, Cicero argued that this use of eloquence will confirm the truth of the philosophy held and identify the orator as "someone polished in all those arts that are proper for a free citizen" (p. 36). From this oratorical foundation, Kimball abstracts an "*artes liberales* ideal" that represented Roman "liberal" education and has influenced later formulations of the term:

> Training citizen-orators to lead society requires identifying true virtues, the commitment to which will elevate the student and the source for which is great texts, whose authority lies in the dogmatic premise that they relate the true virtues, which are embraced for their own sake. (p. 228)

This *artes liberales* ideal might be called an agenda for development of character worthy in its own right, not simply as preparation for vocation, although presumably people so educated will in fact be part of the class (in Roman times) that is leisured and can afford personal development as an end in itself.

This tradition received significant encouragement from early Christian interpreters of the role of the seven liberal arts in the proper study of Scripture. Cassiodorus in the sixth century cited Prov. 9:1—"Wisdom has built a home for herself and hewn out seven columns"—and Exod. 25:37—"You shall make seven lamps and put them so they light out against it"—as evidence for the importance of "human readings" to complement the "divine readings" in monastic educational practice (p. 44). The change that came with medieval Christian thinking concerned the end of education to be not personal refinement, but rather more skillful reading and interpretation of sacred texts of Scripture. Thus the liberal arts became subservient to the study of Scripture (p. 55).

Set over against this *artes liberales* ideal is the philosophical tradition identified by Kimball as the "liberal-free ideal." Derived ultimately from Plato's discursive search for truth, this emphasis altered the role of the trivium in relation to the quadrivium as preparation for the study of philosophy in the medieval university. Thomas Aquinas emphasized logic rather than rhetoric as the heart of the trivium, with grammar reduced to a study of rules for logical constructs rather than a means of promoting rhetoric, and mathematics (and the quadrivium) elevated as a discipline for training the mind to pursue questions of meaning rather than providing basic knowledge towards character formation. Philosophy was divided into three types—natural philosophy, moral philosophy, and metaphysics—all progressively beyond the trivium and quadrivium, leading to the professional study of law (or medicine or religion). This ascendance of the philosophic model curtailed the liberal arts emphasis on rhetoric in favor of pursuit of professional or graduate specialization. Disciplining the mind in the philosophic model reduced the value of liberal arts for their own sake. Thus was born the conflict between vocational education and education for life.

From that early emergence, Kimball traces the growth of the liberal-free model to the New Philosophy and the development of modern science in the Renaissance. He identifies the seeds of the liberal-free model as follows: (1) "an emphasis on freedom, especially from a priori strictures and standards," with Locke and Rousseau as early advocates; (2) "an emphasis on intellect and rationality," seen in Diderot's call for an Age of Reason and in Descartes; (3) "a critical skepticism," with Hume claiming empiricism's inability to obtain certainty; (4) "tolerance" based on skepticism and doubt of absolutes (such as virtues) seen in Locke for example; leading toward (5) egalitarianism as a condition of nature's provision for all men, from Hobbes through Locke and Rousseau, but debunked by Hume; (6) "emphasis upon volition of the individual rather than upon the obligations of citizenship," and therefore concern for individual growth; which produces (7) the belief that individual growth is an end in itself: "Since conclusions are always subject to criticism, it is not the truth that is finally desirable, but the search" (pp. 119-122). Lessing and Kant are cited as examples of this argument.

I have noted the thinkers associated with the liberal-free ideal in order to illustrate Kimball's eclectic methodology. He develops his model by drawing from diverse thinkers who might not agree in particulars but who, in combination, put forward a position which influences how liberal arts are viewed down to the present.

Education in America before and after the Revolution reveals a conflict between *liberal* meaning free or unrestrained, in tension with *liberal* meaning magnanimous or gentlemanly, befitting a person of leisure. Kimball argues for a degree of ambiguity in the term liberal education in order to suit those who defended public education and the study of classical languages in schools against the pressures of professionalism. Experimental sciences, advanced mathematics, and vernacular languages made little headway until after the Civil War as major components in university curricula associated with liberal arts. Among other promoters of change were the land grant institutions that came into existence after 1862 advocating utility and technology.

What happened between the Civil War and World War II can be summed up in Kimball's quoting of John Dewey in 1944 that "liberating" had come to be synonymous with "liberal" in discussions of liberal education, whether for "free men" or to counter specialization with its development of the undergraduate major and minor in support of sciences, specialization, and freedom to teach what one wishes and to study what one wishes (pp. 162-163). One symptom of the erosion of liberal education in the oratorical tradition was the elimination in many schools of the senior-year course in moral philosophy. Kimball identifies this trend with the rise of pragmatism.

Pragmatism by definition resists absolutes and promotes adaptability and individuality, among other things. But Kimball notes a continuing interest in liberal education defined in terms of individualism, egalitarianism, and culture. That is, general education might be about preparing individual students "for life in general according to their particular needs and desires." But it also might mean "all people in general would receive the same education." Or it might suggest that "everyone in general should aspire" to a common education, a "highest common denominator," implying that there are some things all educated people should know—kind of a "universal knowledge" (pp. 194-195).

The final chapter of *Orators and Philosophers* is titled "A Typology of Contemporary Discussion." If you are short of time, you can read here his quick review tracing the historical development of the two opposing traditions and their modifications made under the influence of each other's appeal. In the past half-century of debate, Kimball notes, the *artes liberales* ideal remains skeptical of the liberal-free ideal with its "unconditional, open-ended search for truth" (p. 216). And loudest in criticism of that model are the sectarian schools, which believe that "some truth is known," and therefore values education should be part of what liberal education addresses. Meanwhile, the liberal-free argument continues to be made for enabling fulfillment of the desires and aspirations of the individual (p. 217).

The defining distinction between these two "purist" positions might be as follows: in the *artes liberales* ideal, "a presumption of certitude underlies the identification of virtues and standards reposited in classical texts, and commitment is thereby demanded, identifying an elite who embrace the virtues and preserve them as leaders of society" (p. 218). In contrast, the liberal-free ideal is founded on "skeptical doubt" that "undermines all certainty, casting individuals entirely upon their own intellect for judgments that can never finally be proven true." This leads to tolerance and respect for others' views, with an assumption that "all beliefs must change and develop over time" (p. 219). The curriculum best suited to develop these perspectives includes logic and mathematics for honing the mind, and experimental science which teaches the honed intellect to turn old truths into new hypotheses for further testing" (p. 219).

Perhaps it will be helpful here to insert Kimball's liberal-free ideal in a schema that sets it against the *artes liberales* characteristics described earlier: "(1) Epistemological skepticism underlies (2) the free and (3) intellectual search for truth, which is forever elusive, and so all possible views must be (4) tolerated and given (5) equal hearing (6) with the final decision left to each individual, (7) who pursues truth for its own sake" (p. 228).

The debate continues between the two ideals, with the liberal-free ideal currently dominant. But the *artes liberales* tradition still appeals for "investigation of the best of tradition and the public expression of the good and the true, rather than the discovery of new knowledge," even though this can easily lead to "dogmatic conservation in education and culture," in other words, authoritarianism, precisely what the university has worked so hard to be liberated from (p. 237). On the other hand, the individualistic free pursuit of truth can lead to nihilistic, self-indulgent education and culture, ultimately to anarchy. So what do we do?

Kimball's answer is to seek community, based on a balance between the two ideals, under the ancient Greek concept of *logos*. The philosophic tradition sees *logos* as privileging reason (logic) and mathematics; the oratorical tradition sees *logos* as privileging speech. Therefore a recognition of the healthy tension between reason and speech, both considered essential in defining what it means to be human, and separating us from other orders of creation, should be sought. If community is "a group of people who talk to each other and do it well" (p. 240), then we might establish in our academic institutions the means by which we elevate talking to each other as a necessary corrective to the individualism prevalent on the research/specialization model of education currently dominant. Kimball reminds us that community was dear to Socrates as much as to Cicero: the philosophers valued language and discussion as a way to seek truth as much as the orators who insisted that education be marked by the ability to reason well and express understanding of what was read and thought. Kimball betrays a bias toward the value of submitting to the great texts, "not that truth lies explicitly in the texts, but rather that it emerges through the disciplined effort to understand and express the meaning of the texts" (p. 238). Something of a grand conversation.

End of story? Not quite! Just when one has finished tracking Kimball's "big picture" history of the difference between the tradition favoring reason—"including its various denotations of a rationale, a faculty of thinking, and an act of thinking"—and the tradition favoring speech—"the pronouncing of words, the faculty of talking, and a formal act of communication" (p. 3) in liberal education, and accepted the possibility of some compromise based on the idea of community, Kimball's next essay, *The Condition of American Liberal Education*, opens with the shocking disclosure: "I recant. No, I reconstruct" (p. xxi). What he reconstructs is a view of liberal education in America at the close of the twentieth century that he labels pragmatism. In arguing for the pervasiveness of pragmatism in contemporary liberal education, Kimball identifies six of its tenets which are widely embraced. The "six points of pragmatism" are,

> (1) that belief and meaning, even truth itself, are fallible and revisable; (2) that an experimental method of inquiry obtains in all science and reflective thought; (3) that belief, meaning, and truth depend on the context and the intersubjective judgment of the community in which they are formed; (4) that experience is the dynamic interaction of organism and environment, resulting in a close interrelationship between thought and action; (5) that the purpose of resolving doubts or solving problems is intrinsic to all thought and inquiry; and (6) that all inquiry and thought are evaluative, and judgments about fact are no different from judgments about value. (p. 29)

Kimball also recounts the practical consequences of resurgent pragmatism. He argues there are seven recent developments in liberal education that are best explained on pragmatic grounds:

1. **multiculturalism**, because "belief, meaning, and knowledge depend on perspective and context" (p. 89);
2. **values and service**, because we recognize the importance of moral values and ethics;
3. **community and citizenship**, because we recognize learning takes place in community;
4. **general education**, because formation of values is as important as the search for knowledge, and specialization can be too prone to fragmentation;

5. **commonality and cooperation** between college and other levels of the education system, which was dear to Dewey's heart for reform of society;
6. **teaching as learning and inquiry**, rather than merely transmission of knowledge, so teachers are also involved in the learning process; and
7. **assessment**, because it suggests that reflective inquiry must be tested to see what difference it makes if *this* rather than *that* is taught. (p. 96)

These seven developments are recognizable to anyone involved in discussions of general education during recent years. Whether or not they have their roots in pragmatism is not as important as whether seeing these seven trends suggests a way of establishing the kind of community Kimball had advocated in his previous book as a way to reconcile the opposing tensions between orators and philosophers.

The second half of *The Condition of American Liberal Education* is a series of essays in response to Kimball. Most of them disagree on the uniformity or consistency of these seven trends as a new liberal education model. Because many are written by scholars who have published their own major studies of liberal education in recent years, their views are fascinating but beyond the scope of this review. It is disappointing that none of the respondents represent distinctly sectarian schools to raise the issue of truths that can be known and values that can be posited in reaction against the strictly pragmatic philosophy Kimball holds out as our best hope for consensus in liberal education. Among Christian colleges and universities, I would expect to see several variations on accommodating the professional preparation goal while still arguing for a liberal arts objective of education for life. Skills courses and broad selection of courses in categories rather than narrowly limited core requirements challenge the capacity to create an agreed-upon small group of essential courses all students can be required to complete despite their majors or professional goals. Yet that is a challenge faced by those schools that claim to offer an alternative to the liberal-free or pragmatic modification of the liberal-free ideal. And then, of course, what will happen with the continued evolution of new teaching/learning systems: adult learners, distance education, virtual universities, and other technologically driven changes in how learning takes place and the role of faculty in conveying values education?

What finally is fascinating about the work Kimball has put before us is that there *are* reasons that explain how we got to where we are in general education programs. And there are long-standing philosophical differences that impinge on any individual college's or university's decision to organize and assess the learning activities that comprise general education. In our increasingly complex, interconnected world, the questions may change, but the answers sought echo through the centuries of accommodation and response to change that has always characterized attempts to determine what it means to be educated—to be generally educated, and for what purpose.

Bibliography

Abelson, Paul. *The Seven Liberal Arts: A Study in Medieval Culture*. 2 vols. New York, NY: Teachers College, Columbia University, 1906.

Adler, Mortimer. *How to Read a Book: The Art of Getting a Liberal Education*. New York, NY: Simon and Schuster, 1966.

________. *Reforming Education: The Opening of the American Mind*. New York, NY: Collier Books, Macmillan, 1990.

Alverno College Faculty. *Liberal Learning at Alverno College*. 5th ed. Milwaukee, WI: Alverno Productions, 1992.

American Assembly of Collegiate Schools of Business. *Achieving Quality and Continuous Improvement through Self-Evaluation and Peer Review*. St. Louis, MO: AACSB—The International Association for Management Education, 1994-95.

Anderson, Charles W. *Prescribing the Life of the Mind: An Essay on the Purpose of the University, the Aims of Liberal Education, the Competence of Citizens, and the Cultivation of Practical Reason*. Madison, WI: University of Wisconsin Press, 1993.

Aquinas, Thomas. *Summa Theologica*. Translated by the Fathers of the English Dominican Province. Online. http://www.knight.org/advent/summa/209402.htm.

Aristotle. *Metaphysics*. Translated by W. D. Ross. Online. http://classics.mit.edu/Aristotle/metaphysics.1.i.html

________. *Nicomachean Ethics*. Translated by Martin Ostwald. Englewood, NJ: Prentice Hall, 1962.

________. *The Politics of Aristotle*. Edited and translated by Ernest Barker. Oxford: Clarendon, 1946. Reprint, Oxford: Oxford University Press, 1958. Also available online. Translated by H. Rackham. http://hydra.perseus.tufts.edu/cgi-bin/text?lookup=aristot.+pol.+1252a

Armour, Robert A., and Barbara Schneider Fuhrmann, eds. *Integrating Liberal and Professional Education*. New Directions for Teaching and Learning, no. 40. San Francisco, CA: Jossey-Bass, 1989.

Arnold, Matthew. *Discourses in America*. London: Macmillan, 1885.

Asheville Institute on General Education. *Proceedings: June 7-12, 1991*. Washington, D.C.: Association of American Colleges, 1992.

Association of American Colleges (Project on General Education Models). *General Education: Issues and Resources*. Washington, D.C.: Society for Values in Higher Education and Association of American Colleges, 1980.

________ (Project on Redefining the Meaning and Purpose of Baccalaureate Degrees). *Integrity in the College Curriculum: A Report to the Academic Community*. Washington, D.C.: Association of American Colleges, 1985.

________ (Task Group on General Education). *A New Vitality in General Education*. Washington, D.C.: Association of American Colleges, 1988.

________ (Project on Strong Foundations for General Education). *Strong Foundations: Twelve Principles for Effective General Education Programs*. Washington, D.C.: Association of American Colleges, 1994.

Astone, B., and E. Nunez-Wormack. "Population Trends, Socioeconomic Status, and Geographic Distribution." In *College Students: The Evolving Nature of Research*, edited by F. K. Stage, 4-17. Needham Heights, MA: Simon and Schuster Custom Publishing, 1996.

Augustine, Saint. *On Christian Teaching*. Oxford: Oxford University Press, 1997.

Bacon, Francis. *First Book of Aphorisms*. In *The Age of Reason: The 17th Century Philosophers*, selected and introduced by Stuart Hampshire. New York, NY: Mentor Books, 1956.

________. *New Atlantis*. In *Ideal Commonwealths*. New York, NY: Colonial Press, 1901.

________. *Advancement of Learning and Novum Organum*. New York, NY: Willey, 1900.

Bailyn, Bernard. *Education in the Forming of American Society: Needs and Opportunities for Study*. New York, NY: Vintage Books, 1960.

Balch, Stephen H., and Rita Clara Zurcher, eds. *The Dissolution of General Education: 1914-1993*. Princeton, NJ: National Association of Scholars, 1996.

Baird, David, Thomas G. Bost, Jennifer Farley Brase, Isaac Bright, Mandy Broaddus, Ron Highfield, Douglas Kmiec, D'Esta Love, John Nicks, Cynthia Novak, Don Thompson, and Norman Fischer. *Opportunities for Liberal Learning in the Twenty-First Century*. Malibu, CA: Pepperdine University, 1997.

Beesley, Patricia. *The Revival of the Humanities in American Education*. New York, NY: Columbia University Press, 1940.

Bell, Daniel. *The Reforming of General Education: The Columbia College Experience in Its National Setting*. New York, NY: Columbia University Press, 1966. Reprint, Garden City, NY: Anchor Books, 1968.

Bellah, Robert N., et al. *Habits of the Heart: Individualism and Commitment in American Life*. Berkeley, CA: University of Berkeley, 1985.

________. *The Good Society*. New York, NY: Knopf, 1991.

Bennett, William John. *To Reclaim a Legacy: A Report on the Humanities in Higher Education*. Washington, D.C.: Educational Resources Information Center, Department of Education, 1984.

Bledstein, Burton J. *The Culture of Professionalism: The Middle Class and the Development of Higher Education in America*. New York, NY: W. W. Norton, 1978.

Blinderman, Abraham. *American Writers on Education Before 1865*. Boston, MA: Twayne Publishers, 1975.

Bloland, Harland G. "Postmodernism and Higher Education." *Journal of Higher Education* 66, no. 5 (1995): 521-560.

Bloom, Allan. *The Closing of the American Mind*. New York, NY: Simon and Schuster, 1987.

Blumenstyk, Goldie. "Royalties on Inventions Bring $336-Million to Top U.S. Research Universities." *The Chronicle of Higher Education*, 27 February 1998, A44.

Bolgar, R. R. *The Classical Heritage and Its Beneficiaries*. Cambridge: Cambridge University Press, 1954.

Boli, John, Francisco Ramirez, and John Meyer. "Explaining the Origins and Expansion of Mass Education." *Comparative Education Review* 29, no. 2 (1985): 145-170.

Bonhoeffer, Dietrich. *Letters and Papers From Prison*. London: SCM Press, 1971.

Bonner, Stanley. *Education in Ancient Rome: From the Elder Cato to the Younger Pliny*. Berkeley, CA: University of California Press, 1977.

Bosch, David. *Transforming Mission: Paradigm Shifts in Theology of Mission*. New York, NY: Orbis Books, 1993.

Boyer, Ernest L. *College: The Undergraduate Experience in America*. New York, NY: Harper and Row, 1987.

Boyer, Ernest L., and Arthur Levine. *A Quest for Common Learning: The Aims of General Education*. Princeton, NJ: Carnegie Foundation for the Advancement of Teaching, 1981.

Brann, Eva T. H. *Paradoxes of Education in a Republic*. Chicago, IL: University of Chicago Press, 1979.

Breneman, David. *Liberal Arts Colleges: Thriving, Surviving, or Endangered?* Washington, D.C.: Brookings, 1994.

Burhans, Clinton S., Jr. "The Demise of the Cultural Core: Whatever Happened to General Education?" *Journal of General Education* 36 (1984): 154-66.

Capella, Martianus. *De Nuptiis Philologiae et Mercurii* (The Marriage of Philology and Mercury). Vol. 2 of *Martianus Capella and the Seven Liberal Arts*. William Harris Stahl and Richard Johnson. New York, NY: Columbia University Press, 1971, 1977.

Carnegie Foundation for the Advancement of Teaching. *Missions of the College Curriculum: A Contemporary Review with Suggestions*. San Francisco, CA: Jossey-Bass Publishers, 1978.

Carnochan, William B. *The Battleground of the Curriculum: Liberal Education and the American Experience*. Stanford, CA: Stanford University Press, 1993.

Cassiodorus, Magnus Aurelius. *Institutiones*. Edited by R. A. Mynors. Oxford: Clarendon, 1961.

Cheit, Earl F. *The Useful Arts and the Liberal Tradition*. New York, NY: McGraw-Hill, 1975.

Cheney, Lynne V. *50 Hours: A Core Curriculum for College Students*. Washington, D.C.: National Endowment for the Humanities, 1989.

Clarke, Martin Lowther. *Classical Education in Britain, 1500-1900*. Cambridge: Cambridge University Press, 1959.

________. "The Educational Writings of Erasmus." *Erasmus in English* 8 (1976): 23-31.

________. *Higher Education in the Ancient World*. Albuquerque, NM: University of New Mexico Press, 1971.

Commission on Teacher Credentialing. *California Standards for the Teaching Profession: A Description of Professional Practice for California Teachers*. Sacramento, CA: State of California, 1997.

Commission on the Core Curriculum. *Report of the Commission on the Core Curriculum*. New York, NY: Columbia College, 1988.

Committee on the Objectives of a General Education in a Free Society. *General Education in a Free Society: Report of the Harvard Committee*. Cambridge, MA: Harvard University Press, 1945.

Conn, Robert H. "Rear Guard on the Escalator: The Struggle to Protect the Liberal Arts Core in Higher Education." Occasional Papers, no. 80, Board of Higher Education and Ministry, The United Methodist Church, Nashville, Tenn., October 1989.

Coupland, Douglas. *Generation X: Tales for an Accelerated Culture*. New York, NY: St. Martin's Press, 1991.

Cremin, Lawrence Arthur. *American Education: The Colonial Experience, 1607-1783*. New York, NY: Harper and Row, 1970.

Curtis, Stanley James. *History of Education in Great Britain*. University Tutorial Press, 1948. Reprint, Westport, CT: Greenwood Press, 1953, 1971.

de Rijk, Lambert. "*Enkuklios Paideia*: A Study of Its Original Meaning." *Vivarium* 3 (1965): 24-93.

Derrick, Christopher. *Escape from Scepticism: Liberal Education as if Truth Mattered*. LaSalle, IL: Sherwood Sugden, 1977.

Dewey, John. "Challenge to Liberal Thought." *Fortune*, August 1944, 155-157.

________. *Democracy and Education*. New York, NY: Macmillan. Reprint, New York, NY: Free Press, 1967.

Drucker, Peter F. *Managing in a Time of Great Change*. San Francisco, CA: Jossey-Bass, 1995.

D'Souza, Dinesh. *Illiberal Education: The Politics of Race and Sex on Campus*. New York, NY: Free Press/Macmillan, 1991.

Erasmus, Desiderius. *The Education of a Christian Prince*. Translated with an introduction by Lester K. Born. New York, NY: Columbia University Press, 1936. Reprint, New York, NY: W. W. Norton, 1968.

________. *Ten Colloquies*. Translated by Craig R. Thompson. Indianapolis, IN: Bobbs-Merrill Co., 1957.

Essentials of Baccalaureate Education for Professional Nursing. Washington, D.C.: American Association of Colleges of Nursing, June 1997.

Feeney, Joseph J. "Can a Worldview Be Healed? Students and Postmodernism." *America*, 15 November 1997, 12-16.

Flexner, Abraham. *The American College: A Criticism*. New York, NY: Century, 1908. Reprint, New York, NY: Arno Press, 1969.

Forster, Robert and Elborg Forster, eds. *European Society in the Eighteenth Century: Documentary History of Western Civilization*. New York, NY: Harper and Row, 1969.

Freedman, James O. *Idealism and Liberal Education*. Ann Arbor, MI: University of Michigan Press, 1996.

Gaff, Jerry G. *General Education Today: A Critical Analysis of Controversies, Practices, and Reforms*. San Francisco, CA: Jossey-Bass, 1983.

________. *New Life for the College Curriculum: Assessing Achievements and Furthering Progress in the Reform of General Education*. San Francisco, CA: Jossey-Bass, 1991.

Gaff, Jerry G., James L. Ratcliff, and associates, eds. *The Handbook of the Undergraduate Curriculum: A Comprehensive Guide to Purposes, Structures, Practices and Change*. San Francisco, CA: Jossey-Bass, 1997.

Gamson, Zelda F. "Changing the Meaning of Liberal Education." *Liberal Education* 75, no. 5 (1989): 10-11.

Gamson, Zelda F., and associates. *Liberating Education*. San Francisco, CA: Jossey-Bass, 1984.

Garland, Martha McMackin. "Newman in His Own Day." In *The Idea of a University*, edited by Frank Turner, 265-281. London: Longman, Green, 1899. Reprint, New Haven, CT: Yale University Press, 1996.

Gilbert, Martin. *Winston S. Churchill*. Volume VII, *The Road to Victory, 1941-1945*. Boston, MA: Houghton Mifflin, 1986.

Glassick, Charles E., Mary Taylor Huber, and Gene I. Maeroff. *Scholarship Assessed: Evaluation of the Professoriate*. San Francisco, CA: Jossey-Bass, 1997.

Gless, Darryl J., and Barbara Herrnstein Smith, eds. *The Politics of Liberal Education*. Durham, NC: Duke University Press, 1992.

Goldwin, Robert A., ed. *Higher Education and Modern Democracy: The Crisis of the Few and the Many*. Chicago, IL: Rand McNally, 1967.

Gordon, Robert Aaron, and James Edwin Howell. *Higher Education for Business*. New York, NY: Columbia University Press, 1959.

Grafton, Anthony, and Lisa Jardine. *From Humanism to the Humanities: Education and the Liberal Arts in Fifteenth- and Sixteenth-Century Europe*. Cambridge, MA: Harvard University Press, 1986.

Greene, Theodore M. *Liberal Education Reconsidered*. Cambridge, MA: Harvard University Press, 1954.

Griswold, A. Whitney, ed. *Liberal Education and the Democratic Ideal.* Enlarged edition. New Haven, CT: Yale University Press, 1962.

Grumet, Madeleine R. "Lofty Action and Practical Thoughts: Education with Purpose." *Liberal Education* 81, no. 1 (1995): 4-11.

Gruget, Lee E. "Liberal Education: Our Phrase of Choice." *Liberal Education* 81, no. 2 (1995): 50-52.

Guinness, Os. *The American Hour: A Time of Reckoning and the Once and Future Role of Faith.* New York, NY: Free Press, 1994.

Guthrie, David S. *Mapping the Terrain of Church-Related Colleges and Universities.* New Directions for Higher Education, no. 79. San Francisco, CA: Jossey-Bass, 1992.

Henry, Carl F. H. "The Christian Pursuit of Higher Education." *Faculty Dialogue* 24 (Spring 1995). Journal online. http://www.iclet.org/pub/facdialogue/24/henry24

Hirsch, E. D., Jr. *Cultural Literacy: What Every American Needs to Know.* Boston, MA: Houghton Mifflin, 1987.

Hirst, Paul. "Liberal Education and the Nature of Knowledge." In *Philosophical Analysis and Education*, edited by Reginald D. Archambault, 113-138. New York, NY: Humanities Press, 1965.

Hobbes, Thomas. *The Elements of Law Natural and Politic.* Online. http://socserv2.socsci.mcmaster.ca/~econ/ugcm/3ll3/hobbes/index.html

________. *Leviathan or the Matter, Form and Power of a Commonwealth Ecclesiastical and Civil.* Oxford: Basil Blackwell, 1960.

Hofstadter, Richard, and Wilson Smith, eds. *American Higher Education: A Documentary History.* 2 vols. Chicago, IL: University of Chicago Press, 1961.

Holborn, Hajo. *A History of Modern Germany: 1648-1840.* New York, NY: Knopf, 1968.

Holmes, Arthur F. *The Idea of a Christian College.* Revised ed. Grand Rapids, MI: Eerdmans, 1987.

Hunter, James Davison. *Evangelicalism: The Coming Generation.* Chicago, IL: University of Chicago Press, 1987.

Hutchins, Robert Maynard. *The Higher Learning in America.* New Haven, CT: Yale University Press, 1936. Reprint, with introduction by Harry S. Ashmore, New Brunswick, NJ: Transaction Publishers, 1995.

Huxley, Thomas. *Science and Education.* New York, NY: The Citadel Press, 1964.

The Idea and Practice of General Education: An Account of the College of the University of Chicago. By Present and Former Members of the Faculty. Chicago, IL: University of Chicago Press, 1950.

Jarman, T. L. *Landmarks in the History of Education: English Education as Part of the European Tradition.* London: Cresset Press, 1951.

Jefferson, Thomas. *Writings*. New York, NY: Literary Classics of the United States, 1984.

Johnson, Alvin. *Liberal Education Fact and Fiction*. New York, NY: New School for Social Research, 1945.

Johnston, Joseph S. *Beyond Borders: Profiles in International Education*. Washington, D.C.: Association of American Colleges, American Assembly of Collegiate Schools of Business, 1993.

Kaplan, Robert. "The Coming Anarchy." *The Atlantic Monthly*, February 1994, 44-76.

Kimball, Bruce. "Founders of Liberal Education: The Case for Roman Orators Against Socratic Philosophers." *Teachers College Record* 85 (1983): 225-249.

________. "Liberal vs. Useful Education: Re-evaluating the Historical Appeals to Benjamin Franklin and Aristotle." *Liberal Education* 67, no. 4 (1981): 286-292.

________. "Matthew Arnold, Thomas Huxley, and Liberal Education: A Centennial Retrospective." *Teachers College Record* 86 (1985): 475-487.

________. *Orators and Philosophers: A History of the Idea of Liberal Education*. Expanded edition. New York: Teachers College, Columbia University, 1986. Reprint, New York, NY: College Entrance Examination Board, 1995.

Kolakowski, Leszek. *Modernity on Endless Trial*. Chicago, IL: University of Chicago Press, 1990.

Krieger, Martin H. "Broadening Professional Education on the Margins and Between the Niches." *Liberal Education* 76, no. 2 (1990): 6-10.

Lazerson, Marvin, and W. Norton Grubb, eds. *American Education and Vocationalism: A Documentary History, 1870-1970*. New York, NY: Teachers College, Columbia University, 1974.

Lee, Gordon C. *Education and Democratic Ideals: Philosophical Backgrounds of Modern Educational Thought*. New York, NY: Harcourt, Brace, 1965.

Lewis, C. S. "Christianity and Culture." In *Christian Reflections*. Grand Rapids, MI: Eerdmans, 1994.

Locke, John. *Some Thoughts Concerning Education; and, Of the Conduct of the Understanding*. Indianapolis, IN: Hackett, 1996.

Lucas, Christopher J. *American Higher Education: A History*. New York, NY: St. Martin's Press, 1994.

Lynton, Ernest A. "New Concepts of Professional Expertise: Liberal Learning as Part of Career-Oriented Education." Working paper no. 4, New England Resource Center for Higher Education, Boston, Mass., 1990.

MacIntyre, Alasdair. *After Virtue: A Study in Moral Theory*. Notre Dame, IN: University of Notre Dame Press, 1981.

Malcolmson, Patrick, Richard Myers, and Colin O'Connell. *Liberal Education and Value Relativism: A Guide to Today's B.A.* New York, NY: University Press of America, 1996.

Maritain, Jacques. *Education at the Crossroads*. New Haven, CT: Yale University Press, 1943.

Marrou, Henri. *A History of Education in Antiquity*. Translated by George Lamb. New York, NY: Sheed and Ward, 1956.

Marsden, George. *The Outrageous Idea of Christian Scholarship*. New York, NY: Oxford University Press, 1997.

________. *The Soul of the American University: From Protestant Establishment to Established Nonbelief.* New York, NY: Oxford University Press, 1994.

Marsh, Peter. *Contesting the Boundaries of Liberal and Professional Education: The Syracuse Experiment*. Syracuse, NY: Syracuse University Press, 1988.

Marshall, Paul. *A Kind of Life Imposed on Man: Vocation and Social Order from Tyndale to Locke*. Toronto: University of Toronto Press, 1996.

Martin, Everett Dean. *The Meaning of a Liberal Education*. New York, NY: W. W. Norton, 1926.

McDowell James L. "Increasing the Liberal Arts Content of Professional/ Technical Curriculum." Paper presented at the Annual Conference of the Association for General and Liberal Studies, Daytona Beach, Fla., October 1996.

McGarry, Daniel. "Educational Theory in the *Metalogicon* of John of Salisbury." *Speculum* 23 (1948): 659-675.

McGrath, Earl J. *Liberal Education in the Professions*. New York, NY: Teachers College, Columbia University, 1959.

Meiklejohn, Alexander. *The Liberal College*. Boston, MA: Marshall Jones, 1920.

Milbank, John. *Theology and Social Theory*. Cambridge, MA: Blackwell, 1990.

Miller, Gary E. *The Meaning of General Education: The Emergence of a Curriculum Paradigm*. New York, NY: Teachers College, Columbia University, 1988.

Milton, John. "Of Education." In *Selected Essays of John Milton*, edited by Laura E. Lockwood. Boston, MA: Houghton Mifflin, 1911.

Mitchell, Basil. *Morality, Religious and Secular: The Dilemma of the Traditional Conscience*. Oxford: Clarendon, Oxford University Press, 1980.

More, Sir Thomas. *Utopia*. Online. gopher://gopher.cc.columbia.edu:71/11/ miscellaneous/cubooks/offbooks/more

Morison, Samuel E. *The Founding of Harvard College*. Cambridge, MA: Harvard University Press, 1935.

Mulcaster, Richard. *Positions*. Online. http://www.ucs.mun.ca/˜wbarker/ positions.html

Myers, A. R. *England in the Late Middle Ages*. 8th ed. Middlesex, England: Penguin, 1971.

Nash, Paul, Andreas M. Kazamias, and Henry J. Perkinson, eds. *The Educated Man: Studies in the History of Educational Thought*. New York, NY: John Wiley, 1965.

Nash, Ronald. *The Closing of the American Heart*. Dallas, TX: Probe Books, 1990.

Newbigin, Lesslie. *Foolishness to the Greeks: The Gospel and Western Culture*. Grand Rapids, MI: Eerdmans, 1986.

Newman, John Henry. *The Idea of a University*. Edited by Frank M. Turner. London: Longman, Green, 1899. Reprint, New Haven, CT: Yale University Press, 1996.

Nietzsche, Friedrich. "Thus Spoke Zarathustra." In *The Portable Nietzsche*, translated by Walter Kaufmann. New York, NY: Penguin Books, 1982.

Oakeshott, Michael. *The Voice of Liberal Learning*. Edited by Timothy Fuller. New Haven, CT: Yale University Press, 1989.

Oakley, Francis. *Community of Learning: The American College and the Liberal Arts Tradition*. New York, NY: Oxford University Press, 1992.

Orrill, Robert, ed. *The Condition of American Liberal Education: Pragmatism and a Changing Tradition*. An essay by Bruce A. Kimball with commentaries and responses. New York, NY: College Entrance Examination Board, 1995.

________, ed. *Education and Democracy: Re-imagining Liberal Learning in America*. New York, NY: College Entrance Examination Board, 1997.

Padilla, Rene. *Mission Between the Times*. Grand Rapids, MI: Eerdmans, 1985.

Pangle, Lorraine Smith, and Thomas L. Pangle. *The Learning of Liberty: The Educational Ideas of the American Founders*. Kansas City, KS: University Press of Kansas, 1993.

Pelikan, Jaroslav. *The Idea of the University: A Reexamination*. New Haven, CT: Yale University Press, 1992.

Pew Health Professions Commission. *Healthy America: Practitioners for 2005: An Agenda for Action for U.S. Health Professional Schools*. Durham, NC: Duke Medical Center, 1991.

Pierson, F. C. *The Education of American Businessmen*. New York, NY: McGraw-Hill, 1959.

Plato. *Meno*. Online. http://hydra.perseus.tufts.edu/cgi-bin/text?lookup=plat.+meno+70a

________. *The Republic of Plato*. 2nd ed. Translated by Allan Bloom. New York, NY: Basic Books, 1991.

Porter, Lyman W., and Lawrence E. McKibbin. *Management Education and Development: Drift or Thrust into the 21st Century?* New York, NY: McGraw-Hill, 1988.

Quintilian. *Training of an Orator*. 4 vols. Translated by H. E. Butler. Loeb Classical Library. Cambridge, MA: Harvard University Press, 1920-22.

Rosovsky, Henry. *The University: An Owner's Manual*. New York, NY: W. W. Norton, 1990.

Rothblatt, Sheldon. *Tradition and Change in English Liberal Education: An Essay in History and Culture*. London: Faber and Faber, 1976.

Rousseau, Jean-Jacques. *Emile*. Edited by Allan Bloom. Harmondsworth, England: Penguin, 1991.

Rudolph, Frederick. *The American College and University: A History*. New York, NY: Knopf, 1962. Reprint, Athens, GA: University of Georgia Press, 1990.

________, ed. *Essays on Education in the Early Republic*. Cambridge, MA: Harvard University Press, 1965.

Rudy, Willis. *The Evolving Liberal Arts Curriculum: A Historical Review of Basic Themes*. New York, NY: Teachers College, Columbia University, 1960.

________. *The Universities of Europe 1100-1914: A History*. Cranbury, NJ: Associated University Press, 1984.

Salisbury, John of. *The Metalogicon of John of Salisbury, A Twelfth-Century Defense of the Verbal and Logical Arts of the Trivium*. Translated by Daniel D. McGarry. Berkeley, CA: University of California Press, 1955.

Sample, Steven B. "The Great Straddlers—Successors to the Renaissance Man." *Liberal Education* 81, no. 4 (1995): 54-57.

Schmidt, George. *The Liberal Arts College: A Chapter in American Cultural History*. New Brunswick, NJ: Rutgers University Press, 1957.

Simon, Herbert A. *The Sciences of the Artificial*. Cambridge, MA: MIT Press, 1969.

Smith, J. Winfree. *A Search for the Liberal College: The Beginning of the St. John's Program*. Annapolis, MD: St. John's College Press, 1983.

Smith, Page. *Killing the Spirit: Higher Education in America*. New York, NY: Viking Penguin, 1990.

Smith, Wilson, comp. *Theories of Education in Early America, 1655-1819*. Indianapolis, IN: Bobbs-Merrill, 1973.

Snow, C. P. *The Two Cultures and the Scientific Revolution*. New York, NY: Cambridge University Press, 1961.

Stark, Joan S. "Liberal Education and Professional Programs: Conflict, Coexistence or Compatibility?" In *Creating Career Programs in a Liberal Arts Context*, edited by Mary Ann F. Rehnke, 91-102. New Directions for Higher Education, no. 57. San Francisco, CA: Jossey-Bass, 1987.

Stark, Joan S., and Malcolm A. Lowther. *Strengthening the Ties That Bind: Integrating Undergraduate Liberal and Professional Study*. Report of the Professional Preparation Network. Ann Arbor, MI: Professional Preparation Network, 1988.

Strauss, Leo. "Liberal Education and Responsibility." In *Liberalism: Ancient and Modern*. New York, NY: Basic Books, 1968.

________. "What Is Liberal Education?" In *Liberalism: Ancient and Modern*. New York, NY: Basic Books, 1968.

Taylor, Charles. *Sources of the Self: The Making of the Modern Identity*. Cambridge, MA: Harvard University Press, 1989.

Taylor, Harold. "Individualism and the Liberal Tradition." In *The Goals of Higher Education*, edited by Willis D. Weatherford, Jr. Cambridge, MA: Harvard University Press, 1960.

Thomas, Russell Brown. *The Search for a Common Learning: General Education, 1800-1960*. New York, NY: McGraw-Hill, 1962.

Trueblood, Elton. *The Idea of a College*. New York, NY: Harper and Brothers, 1959.

Useem, Michael. "Corporate Restructuring and Liberal Learning." *Liberal Education* 81, no. 1 (1995): 18-23.

Valli, Linda. "Teaching Moral Reflection: Thoughts on the Liberal Preparation of Teachers." Paper presented at the National Forum of the Association of Independent Liberal Arts Colleges for Teacher Education, Milwaukee, Wis., November 1990.

Van Doren, Mark. *Liberal Education*. New York, NY: Henry Holt, 1943. Reprint, Boston, MA: Beacon Press, 1959.

Veblen, Thorstein. *The Higher Learning in America*. New York, NY: Hill and Wang, 1968.

Wagner, David, ed. *The Seven Liberal Arts in the Middle Ages*. Bloomington, IN: Indiana University Press, 1983.

Weatherford, Willis D. "Commission on Liberal Learning." *Liberal Education* 57, no. 2 (1971): 37-40.

Weber, Max. *The Protestant Ethic and the Spirit of Capitalism*. New York, NY: Charles Scribner, 1958.

Wegener, Charles. *Liberal Education and the Modern University*. Chicago, IL: University of Chicago Press, 1978.

Westbury, Ian, and Alan C. Purves, eds. *Cultural Literacy and the Idea of General Education*. Chicago, IL: National Society for the Study of Education, 1988.

Westminister Larger Catechism. Online. http://www.reformed.org/documents/larger1.html

Whitehead, Alfred North. *The Aims of Education and Other Essays*. New York, NY: Macmillan, 1929.

Williamson, Samuel R. "When Change is the Only Constant: Liberal Education in the Age of Technology." *Educom Review* 31 (November/December 1996): 39-41.

Willis, John E., Jr. "The Post-Postmodern University." *Change* 27, no. 2 (1995): 59-63.

Winter, David G., David C. McClelland, and Abigail J. Stewart. *A New Case for the Liberal Arts*. San Francisco, CA: Jossey-Bass, 1981.

Wise, John. *The Nature of the Liberal Arts*. Milwaukee, WI: Bruce Publishing, 1947.

Woodward, William Harrison. *Desiderius Erasmus Concerning the Aim and Method of Education*. Cambridge, MA: Cambridge University Press, 1904.

________. *Studies in Education During the Age of the Renaissance, 1400-1600*. With a foreword by Lawrence Stone. New York, NY: Teachers College Press, Columbia University, 1967.

Woody, Thomas. *Liberal Education for Free Men*. Philadelphia, PA: University of Pennsylvania Press, 1951.

Index

—T—

—U—

—V—

—W—

—Y—